Our Judicial Oligarchy

By

Gilbert E. Roe

With an introduction by

Robert M. LaFollette

THE LAWBOOK EXCHANGE, LTD.
Clark, New Jersey
2008

ISBN-13: 978-1-58477-772-4
ISBN-10: 1-58477-772-9

The quality of this reprint is equivalent to the quality of the original work.

THE LAWBOOK EXCHANGE, LTD.
33 Terminal Avenue
Clark, New Jersey 07066-1321

Please see our website for a selection of our other publications and fine facsimile reprints of classic works of legal history:
www.lawbookexchange.com

Library of Congress Cataloging-in-Publication Data

Roe, Gilbert E. (Gilbert Ernstein), 1865-1929.
Our judicial oligarchy / Gilbert E. Roe ; [with an introduction by] Robert M. LaFallette.
p. cm.
Originally published: New York : B.W. Huebsch, 1912.
Includes bibliographical references and index.
ISBN-13: 978-1-58477-772-4 (cloth : alk. paper)
ISBN-10: 1-58477-772-9 (cloth : alk. paper)
1. Courts--United States. I. Title.
KF8700.Z9R55 2007
347.73'1--dc22

2006035983

Printed in the United States of America on acid-free paper

Our Judicial Oligarchy

By

Gilbert E. Roe

With an introduction by

Robert M. LaFollette

New York
B. W. Huebsch
1912

PRINTED IN U. S. A.

INTRODUCTION

The judiciary alone, of all our institutions of government, has enjoyed for many years almost complete freedom from hostile criticism. Until very recently, this branch of our government stood above the legislative and executive departments in popular esteem. Unresponsive, and unresponsible to the public the courts dwelt in almost sacred isolation.

Within the last two or three years the public has begun to turn a critical eye upon the work of the judges. The people in their struggle to destroy special privilege and to open the way for human rights through truly representative government, found barrier after barrier placed across the way of progress by the courts. Gradually the judiciary began to loom up as the one formidable obstacle which must be overcome before anything substantial could be accomplished to free the public from the exactions of oppressive monoplies and from the domination of property interests. A new problem entered into the movement toward democracy — the problem of removing the dead hand of precedent from the judiciary and infusing into it the spirit of the times. So the people, in their need, dropped the unquestioning veneration which custom had fostered as a shield for the judges, and began to examine into the tendencies and practices of the courts.

Such an examination is certain to have a wholesome effect. Courts should have no more to fear from honest criticism than do the Congress and the President. Judges are public servants. Their acts are public acts. In a self-governing nation, neither courts nor their decisions can properly remain above and beyond the control of the sovereign citizens. Judges cannot perform their high function in the public interest unless they are made acquainted with public needs and are responsive to the public will.

The judiciary has grown to be the most powerful institution in our government. It, more than any other, may advance or retard human progress. Evidence abounds that, as constituted to-day, the courts pervert justice almost as often as they administer it. Precedent and procedure have combined to make one law for the rich and another for the poor. The regard of the courts for fossilized precedent, their absorption in technicalities, their detachment from the vital, living facts of the present day, their constant thinking on the side of the rich and powerful and privileged classes have brought our courts into conflict with the democratic spirit and purposes of this generation. Moreover, by usurping the power to declare laws unconstitutional and by presuming to read their own views into statutes without regard to the plain intention of the legislators, they have become in reality the supreme law-making and law-giving institution of our government. They have taken to themselves a power it was never intended they should exercise; a power greater than that entrusted to the courts of any other enlightened nation. And because this tremendous power has been so generally exercised on the side of the wealthy and powerful few, the courts have become at last the strongest bulwark of special privilege. They have come to constitute what may indeed be termed a "judicial oligarchy."

Sensing this, the people have become distrustful. In various ways they have shown their dissatisfaction with the work of the courts. Severe attacks have been made recently upon the integrity and ability of certain judges. Everywhere there is a growing public demand for a change that will bring the judiciary again into its proper sphere and into closer communion with the progressive ideals of this generation.

Mr. Roe's book, "Our Judicial Oligarchy," is a most timely and welcome contribution to this discussion. It stands alone in its analysis of the causes that have led up to the present unsatisfactory status of the courts. Mr. Roe lets the decisions themselves tell the story. He does not "muckrake" the judges. He feels that our problem to-day is not merely one of bad and corrupt judges; but rather one of "conservative," technicality-ridden judges who are seeking to apply to modern conditions the principles of the ancient law. Bad judges may be ousted; "good" judges, unless held to account, may go on thwarting our efforts to bring about social and economic justice. Alone among those who have written on this subject, Mr. Roe has held up to public inspection the acts of the courts, as of more significance than the individual characters of the judges. That is one reason why his book is valuable. When we are questioning the tendency of our courts, we must draw our answers from the most illuminating source, and that naturally lies in the judicial decisions.

With mind trained to the law but with vision unobscured by its technicalities, Mr. Roe has drawn from decisions covering a long period of years those doctrines and rules that have become the guide of our courts. This he does simply, clearly, comprehensively, dispassionately, logically, convincingly. He leaves the reader in full possession of the facts, from which he may draw his own conclusions. He makes no attacks on the courts, unless to quote their own decisions can be construed into an attack. He devotes himself to our system of laws rather than to the individuals who made the laws. He clearly points out the dangers to our institutions found in the present attitude of the courts and suggests a rational remedy.

From long and intimate association with Mr. Roe, I may speak with assurance of his especial fitness to present this important subject adequately and constructively. At one time he was my partner in the practice of law at Madison, Wisconsin. Later, when I left the law to enter public service, Mr. Roe went to New York. He has succeeded by personal force and superior mentality in attaining a leading and independent position at the bar of that city. He has always looked upon the profession of law as one that involves to a high degree responsibility to the public, and it would be difficult to find a successful practitioner who combines with his legal skill a keener sense of duty to the public good. The progressive cause has found in him an able and unwavering champion. Throughout the long contests in Wisconsin and more recently in the nation, I have found him ever ready to make personal sacrifices when there was need for his wide knowledge, his splendid judgment and his fearless and uncompromising spirit. In writing this book, he has carried out consistently his high ideals of service.

"Our Judicial Oligarchy" is a thought-provoking book. Its subject-matter will doubtless make it of especial interest to lawyers and judges, but its readers will not, and should not, be confined to the legal profession. I know of no other volume that is so helpful to an understanding of the problems forced upon us by the courts. I know of no other discussion that contains saner or more constructive suggestions for solving those problems. The clearness of its style and the simplicity with which it handles technical cases, make the book, even to the reader not versed in the law, as interesting as it is illuminating. I wish a copy of this book could be placed in the hands of every citizen of the United States. This book will contribute much to the wise, wholesome, constructive work that must be done in order to reverse the reactionary trend of judicial decisions and to bring the courts abreast of the progressive ideals that are transforming all our other institutions of government.

ROBERT M. LA FOLLETTE.

WASHINGTON, D. C.,
March, 1912.

CONTENTS

CHAPTER IV

WHY THE PEOPLE DISTRUST THE COURTS

CHAPTER V

WHY THE PEOPLE DISTRUST THE COURTS

CHAPTER VI

DANGERS OF POPULAR DISTRUST OF COURTS

CHAPTER VII

SUGGESTIONS CONCERNING REFORMS IN THE JUDICIARY

OUR JUDICIAL OLIGARCHY

CHAPTER I

POPULAR DISTRUST OF THE COURTS

"Every person is entitled to a certain remedy in the law for all injuries or wrongs which he may receive in his person, property or character; he ought to obtain justice freely and without being obliged to purchase it; completely and without denial, promptly and without delay, conformably to the laws." [1]

THE above quoted declaration is found in substance in the constitution or bill of rights of every State in the Union. It is now nearly seven hundred years since the principle of this declaration took concrete form in Magna Charta. It has been established and defended at the cost of bloody revolutions on two continents. It is the foundation of government for all English-speaking people. It is peculiarly dear to the people of the United States. A suspicion in the popular mind that this great declaration was being violated, either in its letter or

[1] Sec. 9, Art. I, Declaration of Rights, forming part of the Constitution of the State of Wisconsin.

its spirit, would be a cause for alarm; while the conviction by a large number of our people that it was being disregarded would be a menace to existing institutions. That such a conviction does exist to-day in the minds of millions of our citizens, and that the ranks of those so believing are being constantly augmented, is a fact easy of proof. State the proposition, that every person has a certain remedy in the law for any injury or wrong that he may suffer, and scores of instances will come to your mind of wrongs wholly unredressed. That one may obtain justice freely, or promptly, or according to the rules of law, rather than according to the will of a Judge is not likely to be asserted to-day by any one familiar with the operation of our courts.

President Taft, in a speech delivered in Chicago on September 16, 1909, and reported in the public press of that city, said:

> "Of all the questions that are before the American people, I regard no one as more important than this; to-wit: The improvement of the administration of justice. We must make it so that the poor man will have as nearly as possible an equal opportunity in litigating as the rich man; and under present conditions, ashamed as we may be of it, this is not the fact."

In his Message to the Sixty-first Congress, under date of December 17, 1909, President Taft substantially repeats the above quoted statement, and further says that the deplorable conditions in the administration of the law are —

"receiving the attention of the Committee of the American Bar Association and of many State bar associations, as well as the considered thought of judges and jurists."

Hon. Walter Clark, Chief Justice of the Supreme Court of North Carolina, recently said:

"At the present time the supreme power is not in the hands of the people, but in the power of the judges, who can set aside at will any expression of the people's will made through an Act of Congress or a State Legislature. These judges are not chosen by the people, nor subject to review by them. This is arbitrary power, and the corporations have taken possession of it simply by naming a majority of the judges." [2]

It is to be remembered that the last person to hear of hostile criticism of the courts is the judge, and next to the judge, the lawyer. It is never for the interests of a lawyer to tell a judge that his decisions are popularly regarded with disfavor, nor is it always safe for him to do so even in the line of his duty. This is well illustrated by an incident which occurred in an Appellate Court in New York City recently, and is reported in the public press of that city under date of February 4, 1911. From that

[2] *The Arena* for November, 1907.

report it appears that a reputable attorney, of many years' practice at the bar, filed a brief, in which he said:

"Simply because he (the opposing counsel), before a young judge who rules sometimes erroneously, and has been, so appellant has been informed, reversed by this court many times, some of his rulings being very flagrant," and so forth.

For this statement he was arraigned at the bar of the court for contempt, and to him the presiding judge said:

"Your being a man of mature years makes your offense more aggravating. In this brief you have, without cause, unjustly assailed a justice of a court. The time has come when notice will be served upon lawyers that every judge of every court must be respected. As far as I am concerned I think you have made no excuse whatever for this unwarranted attack. You can gain nothing by criticising the court."

The foregoing, I think is a fair statement of the attitude of the courts toward criticism of its members. The same Appellate Court, a short time before, had, according to the syllabus of the case, thus characterized the same trial Court:

"Where the Court, upon the trial of a cause therein, quarrels with the counsel for the defendant, gives him no opportunity to interpose objections to questions asked witnesses by the Court, characterizes his objections as ridiculous, refuses to note an exception he has taken, assumes to deny a motion to strike out testimony taken upon the examination of a witness by the Court before the counsel had made such a motion, and threatens to commit him for contempt in the presence of a Jury, such conduct on the part of the trial Court calls for a reversal of a judgment entered upon a verdict in favor of the plaintiff." [3]

It is not surprising, therefore, that neither lawyers nor laymen are anxious to remind courts of their mistakes; and popular discontent with the judiciary must indeed have become formidable in order to have penetrated the ranks of lawyers and even of the judges themselves.

The recent so-called "attacks" of Mr. Roosevelt upon the courts in his speeches during the last few months as published in the press of the country [4] are of great significance, as indicating the esteem or lack of esteem the people at the present time have for the courts.

In a speech before the Colorado Legislature, as re-

[3] Bennett v. Harris, 68 Misc. (N. Y.) 503. For a case in which an attorney was disbarred for a criticism of a judge who was a candidate for reëlection, see in re Thatcher, 80 Ohio St. 492. The Legislature subsequently reinstated Mr. Thatcher, and his case is discussed in a subsequent chapter.

[4] See *New York Times* under date of Aug. 30, 1910 and other papers.

ported, Mr. Roosevelt speaking of two recent decisions of the Supreme Court said:

"If such decisions as these two indicated the court's permanent attitude, there would be really a grave cause for alarm, for such decisions if consistently followed up, would upset the whole system of popular government."

He further refers to such decisions as being "flagrant and direct contradictions to the spirit and needs of the times."

Whether Mr. Roosevelt is right or wrong, is not the question. No man in this country has the genius for detecting public sentiment that Mr. Roosevelt has; and no man believes less in the utility of taking a position unsupported by public sentiment. The universal approval of Mr. Roosevelt's position by plain citizens shows that, as usual, he read aright the popular mind.

The *Appeal to Reason* is a newspaper published in Girard, Kansas. Its list of subscribers already amounting to about half a million, according to the paper's statement of its circulation, has been increasing with great rapidity. Yet this paper's most successful campaign for subscriptions and popular support was based practically upon the savage attacks it made upon the Federal judiciary. The sentence of the editor of the paper imposed by the Federal District Court and affirmed by the Circuit Court of Appeals, to six months' imprisonment and the payment of a fine of $1,500.00 for violation of a postal law (Warren v. U. S., 183 Fed. 718), was commuted on February 1st, 1911, by President Taft, to a fine of $100.00 to be collected only in a civil suit. In commenting on the sentence, President Taft, as reported in the public press at the time, is stated to have said:

"The District Court evidently looked beyond the record of the evidence in this case and found that Warren was the editor and publisher of a newspaper engaged in a crusade against society and government.

"Moreover, this is not a prosecution for criminal libel; it is a prosecution for what at best is the violation of a regulation as to the use of mails. To visit such an offense with a severe punishment is likely to appear to the public to be an effort to punish the defendant for something that could not be charged in the indictment."[5]

There are no doubt some who will consider the language of the President above quoted as a more severe criticism of the court than anything ever said of it by the editor of the *Appeal to Reason,* and its weight is not lessened by the fact that it obviously was not intended as a reflection upon the court.

All political parties in the campaign of 1908, recognized in their platforms the necessity for condemning the recent usurpation of power by the courts.

[5] See press reports of the pardon under date of February 2, 1911.

I give in a footnote the material provisions of the Republican and Democratic platforms on this subject.[6] The platform of the other political parties condemned the Republican and Democratic parties on this subject as not going far enough.

The Socialist Party, casting half a million votes, in its platform for 1908, declared " our courts " are " in the hands of the ruling classes."

The platform of the Independence Party, adopted at Chicago July 28, 1908, contains this:

"The Independence Party condemns the arbitrary use of the writ of injunction and contempt proceedings

6 *Republican Platform:* " We believe, however, that the rules of procedure in the federal courts with respect to the issuance of the writ of injunction should be more accurately defined by the statute, and that no injunction, or temporary restraining order, should be issued without notice except where irreparable injury would result from delay, in which case a speedy hearing thereafter should be granted."

The Democratic Platform: " Experience has proved the necessity and we reiterate the pledge of our National Platforms of 1896 for a modification of the present law relating to injunctions, and 1904 in favor of the measure which passed the United States Senate in 1896, but which a Republican Congress has ever since refused to enact; relating to contempts in federal courts and providing for trial by jury in cases of indirect contempt.

" Questions of judicial practice have arisen, especially in connection with industrial disputes. We deem that the parties to all judicial proceedings should be treated with rigid impartiality, and that injunctions should not be issued in any cases in which injunctions would not issue if no industrial dispute were involved."

as a violation of the fundamental American right of trial by jury. From the foundation of our government down to 1872 the Federal judiciary act prohibited the use of any injunction without reasonable notice, usually after a hearing. We assert that in all actions growing out of a dispute between employers and employés concerning terms or conditions of employment, no injunction should issue until after a trial upon the merits, that such trial should be held before a jury, and that in no case of alleged contempt should any person be deprived of liberty without a trial by jury."

The platform of the People's Party, adopted at St. Louis, April 3, 1908, contained this:

"We condemn all unjust assumption of authority by inferior Federal Courts in annulling by injunction the laws of the States, and demand legislative acts by Congress which will prohibit such usurpation and will restrict to the Supreme Court of the United States the exercise of power in cases involving State Legislation."

Since 1908, State platforms of political parties have in many instances gone further in condemning the usurpation of power by the courts than those above quoted. The constitutions of new States recently admitted to the Union evidence the same thing. For example, the Oklahoma constitution provides for a jury trial in cases of contempt of court; and the proposed Constitution of Arizona accepted by the people by an overwhelming majority but vetoed by the President contained a clause providing for the "recall" of judges.

Miss Jane Addams, the great sociological authority, who certainly is conservative in act and speech, says:

"From my experience I should say perhaps that the one symptom among working men which most distinctly indicates a class feeling is a growing distrust of the integrity of the courts, the belief that the present judge has been a corporation attorney, that his sympathies and experience and his whole view of life is on the corporation's side."[7]

In the City of New York during the early months of 1911 there was held what is called a Child's Welfare Exhibit, meaning an exhibit which shows the conditions under which the children of the less fortunate classes live. It was a most conservative and benevolent undertaking, conducted by most conservative and benevolent people. Tremendous crowds were in attendance upon it constantly for weeks. Prominent among its exhibits was a quotation from an opinion of the Court of Appeals of the State of New York.[8] The history of the case is as follows: In 1884 the Legislature of the State of New York passed an Act entitled "An Act to Improve the Public Health by Prohibiting the Manufacture of Cigars and the preparation of Tobaccos in any form in Tenement Houses in certain cases," etc.

[7] 13 *American Journal of Sociology*, p. 772.

[8] Matter of Application of Jacobs, 98 N. Y. 98, 113.

The Court of Appeals, in the case cited, held this law unconstitutional, and in the opinion used the language prominently displayed in letters nearly a foot long, in the Child's Welfare Exhibit; the language is as follows:

"It cannot be conceived how the cigar maker is to be improved in his health or his morals by forcing him from his home and its hallowed association and beneficent influences to ply his trade elsewhere."

Under this quotation in the Child's Welfare Exhibit was the statement, in equally large letters: "*This decision has blocked effective tenement house legislation up to the present.*"

That the decision of its highest court should be held up to the scorn and contempt of the people of the State by the exceedingly conservative and philanthropic persons managing this Exhibit is very significant; and the remarks that I heard made by those who read the placard were not less so.

President Hadley of Yale University in a recent article entitled, "The Constitutional Position of Property in America" had this to say:

"The general status of the property owner under the law cannot be changed by the action of the legislature or the executive, or the people of a State voting at the polls, or all three put together. It cannot be changed without either concensus of opinion among judges which should lead them to retrace their old views, or an amendment of the Constitution of the United States by the slow and cumbersome machinery provided for that purpose, or, last — and I hope most improbable — a revolution." [9]

Concerning President Hadley's article, *The Independent* in the same issue by the way of editorial comment said:

"Among the multiplying signs of change, President Hadley's keen analysis in *The Independent* of this week of the constitutional position of property in America is one that cannot pass unnoticed. It will not be ignored by the beneficiaries of privilege, nor by the plain man who is allowed to vote, so long as we have Supreme Courts to prevent his vote from doing harm to property rights.

"What millions of plain men have inarticulately felt, President Hadley has turned into clean-cut phrases that will live for many a day. A state of affairs which plain men have felt the increasing pressure of, without being able to understand why, in a republic, the task of contending against it should turn out to be almost hopeless, President Hadley has explained so simply and so clearly that no citizen with any intelligence at all can fail to see precisely what it is that democracy in America is up against."

Delos F. Wilcox, Ph. D., in *The Independent* of October 22, 1908, referring to the Hadley article said:

[9] *The Independent* of April 16, 1910.

"As a matter of fact it is not Bryan or Roosevelt or Lincoln Steffens or Charles Edward Russell that is the revolutionist; these men talk; the Supreme Court of the United States acts. . . . Who are these judges who may not be criticized by the humble citizens from whom in theory all the powers of government, judicial as well as legislative and executive, emanate? In the first place they are lawyers, though not always good ones. . . . The truth is that all kinds of men occupy the bench, among them men who secured their positions through all the different degrees of political chicanery practiced in American politics. Judges appointed for life, having no fear of the power of the people or of the executive to rebuke them, are likely to interpret the law according to their own interests and sympathies, whatever they may be."

At the Governors' conference, held in Spring Lake, N. J., September 14th, 1911, a remarkable arraignment of the Judiciary was made by Hon. Chester H. Aldrich, Governor of Nebraska, and the action of the Governor, in criticizing Federal Judge Sanborn for the decision in the Minnesota rate case, hereafter discussed, was so far approved by the Conference, that it appointed a committee to appear before the Supreme Court when that case was presented on appeal. Among other things, Governor Aldrich said:

"Therefore, I say, that when any court, whether it be the United States Supreme Court or a court of inferior jurisdiction, continually makes effort by a judicial decision to do that which the people and the people alone have a right to do, then I say that such a court is seeking to establish judicial tyranny.

"And if allowed to proceed unchallenged along the line of this unwarranted assumption of power, representative government will simply be that in name only."

Again in the same address, Governor Aldrich, referring to the Sanborn decision, said:

"But here is a court opinion that goes out of its way to bring in isolated instances, and totally ignores the weight of authority wherein it has been held in some leading cases by our Supreme Court that a State railway commission may compel interstate trains to stop at certain stations within a State or may change its time schedule to make connection with other trains and many other things of a like nature. These seem to have been conveniently forgotten by the learned judge in the Minnesota case."

Again, in the same address, he said:

"Probably a whole lot of this trouble comes from the fact that in many instances these inferior courts are composed of lawyers who owe their position, not so much to legal attainment and profound learning, as they do to political service rendered. That explains why in so many instances these court opinions sound very like the argument of a lawyer who holds the brief of a railroad company, rather than an important influential and powerful position at the hands of the judicial system of our country."

I could fill many pages with quotations such as the foregoing from the most thoughtful and intelligent men and women of the country. I have carefully refrained from referring to the open hostility existing at the present time between the courts and organized labor. I have quoted none of the denunciations of the courts which fill what are called class or radical publications. But it is not to be forgotten that the readers and supporters of such publications are numbered by the millions. I have not referred to the fact that in a large class of cases of individuals against corporations, the whole struggle of the defendant is to have the case taken from the Jury by the Judge, while the plaintiff asks no more than that the Jury be given a chance to pass upon the facts. The Judge and Jury in this class of cases mutually distrust each other and the result is, since the power is with the Judge, that Juries have ceased to be independent triers of the facts. Recently I heard a Federal Judge say from the bench, that in all his years of service as a Judge, there had never been but one verdict rendered in his Court contrary to his views. I have not referred to the many attempts made by Congress and State Legislatures in recent years to correct by statute the injustice of judicial decisions, nor to the fact that such attempts have been largely rendered abortive by the action of the courts in declaring such laws invalid. These matters will be considered in subsequent chapters. I have here merely gathered together a few of the evidences of the sober and conservative public sentiment on this question which indicates that we may be in the dilemma suggested by President Hadley where the work of the courts must be undone either by constitutional amendments, or by the courts themselves overturning their own decisions, or finally, as President Hadley suggests, — a revolution.

CHAPTER II

WHY THE PEOPLE DISTRUST THE COURTS

(A) The Courts have usurped the power to declare laws unconstitutional.

STARTING from the same point — The Constitution of the United States — the people and the federal courts have been traveling in opposite directions for more than a hundred years. The State courts at first with some hesitation, have in the main followed the lead of the federal courts. While the people have been remaking the Constitution so as to obtain more complete and immediate control of their government, the courts have been remaking the Constitution so as to escape more completely from popular control. While the people have been laying the foundation for democracy, the courts have been building an oligarchy.

We have but to compare the share in government which the Constitution assigned to the people, and that which they actually possess to-day, to see how radical is the change which has been made in a few years. When the Constitution was adopted in 1787, there was no such thing as manhood suffrage in the colonies. The right to vote or hold office was dependent on property qualifications.[1] Both Daniel Webster and Chancellor Kent viewed with alarm the prospect that freehold property should cease to be the foundation of government, and it was not until the Constitutions of the Western States were adopted after 1816 that manhood suffrage became the rule.[2] To-day not only is manhood suffrage practically universal[3] but the women in many of the States are now admitted to suffrage on equal terms with men, and the movement to extend suffrage to women is everywhere steadily progressing. By the terms of the Constitution, property in the form of slaves was given representation in the government. Since that time the slaves have been not only freed, but given the ballot. When the Constitution was adopted so little was thought of the people's ability to govern themselves that the framers of that instrument provided that the President should be elected by a college of electors, designed to act independently of the will of the people. Carrying out the idea of the distrust of the masses, the Constitution provided for the

[1] *The American Nation, A, History* (A. B. Hart, Editor), Vol. IX, p. 150.

[2] *Id.*, Vol. XIV, pp. 175–6.

[3] All states abolished property qualifications before Rhode Island did so, but that state finally dropped that qualification in 1888. There are now merely some minor tax qualifications in a few of the states, and some very elementary educational qualifications. *Id.*, Vol. XXVI, p. 3.

election of United States Senators by the legislatures of the several States. The people without formally amending the Constitution, have rendered nugatory the provision for the election of the President by an electoral college, and have substituted therefor a direct popular vote. Equally dead in a number of the States is the Constitutional provision respecting the election of United States Senators by legislatures, and it now seems certain that every state will, in the near future, select its Senators by direct vote of the people, whether a formal amendment to the Constitution on the subject is adopted or not.[4]

Great as these changes are, however, they are insignificant in their effect on popular government, compared with the tremendous consequences involved in the laws providing for the Secret Ballot, and

[4] California, Missouri, Nebraska, Oregon and Wisconsin have all provided by law, during the last few years, for a popular vote on candidates for the United States Senate. A measure has many times in recent years passed the House of Representatives by the necessary two-thirds majority, to amend the Constitution so as to elect Senators by popular vote, but such measure was never brought to a vote in the United States Senate until February, 1911, and while it failed of the necessary two-thirds majority, fifty-four Senators voted in favor of it, and only thirty-three against it. Con. Rec., Feb. 28, 1911, p. 3787. On June 12, 1911, the United States Senate voted in favor of a constitutional amendment, providing for the direct election of United States Senators. The House had previously voted favorably on the same proposition, but since the resolution was amended by the Senate, it had to go to conference, and so for the time being failed of passage.

Direct Primaries, and for the Initiative, Referendum and Recall.[5]

It is hardly worth while to make up the roll of States in which these various reforms have been adopted, for by the time the list is completed other States will be added. There has been more fundamental legislation in favor of popular government enacted in the last fifteen years than in all the previous history of the country, and that which has already been adopted is only a small part of the programme now pending.[6] It is to be remembered that the mass of people are always much in advance of their political representatives in a movement toward democracy, so that the legislation already en-

[5] More than one-half the states at the close of 1911 had direct primaries, all adopted in recent years. The Initiative and Referendum have been lately adopted in California, Colorado, Maine, Missouri, Wisconsin and Montana. Michigan has the Initiative and Referendum on amendments to the Constitution. Utah adopted a Constitution providing for Initiative and Referendum in 1900, but the legislature has thus far avoided enacting a law to put it into effect. California, South Dakota, Wisconsin and Washington already have the recall.

[6] The National Progressive Republican League was organized January 21, 1911. Among its organizers are 9 leading United States Senators and 13 leading members of the House of Representatives and 6 governors of states. This organization has for its avowed purpose not only the election of United States Senators by popular vote, but the establishment of the Initiative, Referendum, Recall, Direct Primaries, Corrupt Practice Acts, and other democratic legislation throughout the country.

acted is not the highwater mark of the popular demand. Even the most radical of the men of 1787 who participated in the formation of the Constitution never dreamed of a government wherein the people possessed such powers as the people of this country now exercise, and the Constitution was clearly framed with a view of preventing the exercise of such powers by the masses. Impelled by the spirit of democracy, the people of this country have found ways to avoid the Constitution and possess themselves of the instruments of government.

But this is only a small part of the story. Immediate control of the machinery of government is a means, not an end. The people demand the Initiative and Referendum because they wish to make or unmake laws. They demand the right to recall their representatives, because they are determined that those representatives shall at all times obey the popular will. The injustice of the old laws made plain by knowledge and experience is to be corrected; and the new problems, which are the greatest that ever confronted any people in the history of the world, must also be met. The people have decided that they can do this work for themselves, and have entered upon it. The tradition of the ages, which obtained when the Constitution was adopted, that the people must be protected against themselves by the wealth and intelligence and better element of the community is exploded. No man could now be the candidate of any party for any position who maintained such a dogma.

The relation of the individual to his government has been changed much more in this country since the adoption of the Constitution than it was by its adoption. Greater reforms in government have resulted from the peaceful methods of the last quarter of a century than were accomplished by the American Revolution.

Of all the agencies of government the courts alone have shown themselves insensible of, or indifferent to, this charge. The differences between the people and their courts to-day do not arise, as on some occasions in the past, over a single decision. The differences are more fundamental and far reaching than those which arose at the time of the Dred Scott decision. The courts are frankly the champions of the old order as against the new. They stand for the "sacred rights of property" as against "individual rights." Their decisions, it is charged, are protecting special privilege, and represent ideas of government and of law which are in conflict with the convictions of a majority of the people. Either those decisions must go down and cease to be law, or the forces of democracy and popular rule must be turned back. Which shall it be?

There are three principle grounds of complaint against the courts.

First, that they have usurped the power to declare statutes unconstitutional, and therefore, invalid.

Second, that having seized the power to declare some statutes invalid, because unconstitutional, the courts have come to legislate generally, by declaring other statutes invalid merely because they doubted the wisdom or the justice of such laws, and by reading their own opinions into other statutes regardless of the legislative intention.

Third, that the poor man is not on an equality with the rich one before the courts.

That the courts of this country exercise the power to declare any statute invalid which appears to them in conflict with the Constitution is, of course, admitted. A single individual, if only he hold judicial office, may destroy a most excellent law desired by practically all the people, duly passed by large majorities in both Houses of Congress, and approved by the President. This has been done again and again within the last few years. So far as really important legislation is concerned, such as that relating to taxation, commerce, labor, corporations, trusts and the like, Congress has become little more than a body to initiate or propose legislation. The real power to declare whether that shall be law which Congress and the President have enacted into law, is exercised by the courts. Whether the Constitution conferred this power upon the courts, or whether they have simply assumed it without Constitutional authority, and contrary to the intention of the framers of that document, becomes a pertinent question in view of the agitation at the present time to deprive the courts of such power, or at least, to very materially modify it. It is within the scope of this work only to suggest the leading facts upon which this question turns.

In the first place it is to be noted that the courts of no other country claim the right to set aside the laws made by the legislative branch of the Government. In England, of course the Constitution is unwritten, but that fact would seem to be an argument in favor of the exercise of such power by the courts, rather than against it, for where the Constitution is written so that it may be read as well by one department of the government as another, there would seem to be less excuse than otherwise for lodging the exclusive right to finally interpret the Constitution in one branch of the government to the exclusion of the others. At all events, however, France, Germany and Switzerland, and our sister republics on this Continent, and indeed most countries have written Constitutions and in none of them do the courts claim the prerogative of invalidating laws merely because they may think such laws conflict with the constitution. It is to be remembered also that the Federal Government has only such powers as are delegated to it.[7] It is not pretended that there is any language in the Constitution which expressly gives to the Judiciary more than to the Executive or Legislative branches of the government, power to determine that a law is in conflict with the Constitution. While the proceedings of the Constitutional Convention were secret, we know from Mr. Madison's *Journal* of that Convention, first published in 1839 and then under the authority of the United States Government, and many years after the death of all the participants in the Convention, that no motion was made in the Convention to give the courts power to declare unconstitutional any legislative act duly passed and approved by the executive. Mr. Madison himself did move that the *Supreme Court* in conjunction with the President be given the less objectionable authority to pass upon legislation before it was finally adopted, and if the Supreme Court should hold it unconstitutional, make it necessary that the measure in question be passed by a two-thirds vote of each House before it would become effective as law. This motion was three times made in the Constitutional Convention and three times voted down. Mr. Madison's *Journal* shows the following entries concerning the discussion on this subject:

"Mr. Mercer disapproved of the doctrine that the judges as expositors of the Constitution should have au-

[7] Tenth Amendment in force Dec. 15, 1791, Martin v. Hunter, 1 Wheaton, 326.

thority to declare a law void. He thought laws should be well and carefully made, and then be uncontrollable."[8]

"Mr. Dickinson was strongly impressed with the remark of Mr. Mercer as to the power of the judges to set aside law. . . . The Justiciary of Arragon he observed became by degrees the lawgiver."[9]

Mr. Madison himself some years after the Constitution was adopted, declared in Congress that a decision of a Constitutional question

"may come with as much propriety from the legislature as any other department of Government."[10]

Again,

"I beg to know upon what principle it can be contended that any one department draws from the Constitution greater powers than another in making out the limits of the powers of the several departments."[11]

Again he said:

"Nothing has as yet been offered to invalidate the doctrine that the meaning of the Constitution may as

[8] Vol. IV, pp. 208–9, writings of James Madison as edited by Gaillard Hunt.

[9] *Id.*, p. 210.

[10] Elliot's Debates, Vol. IV, p. 354 (House of Representatives).

[11] *Id.*, p. 382.

well be ascertained by the legislature as by the judicial authority."[12]

John Marshall, before he became chief justice, declared before the Supreme Court of the United States:

"The legislative authority of any Country can only be restrained by its own municipal Constitution; this is a principle that springs from the very nature of society, and the judicial authority can have no right to question the validity of a law unless such a jurisdiction is expressly given by the Constitution."[13]

This certainly was a logical argument, and when the framers of the Constitution desired to give the federal courts power to decide a state statute or Constitution invalid because in conflict with the federal Constitution, or the laws made in pursuance thereof, or treaties made under the authority of the United States, the power so to do was expressly given.[14]

It can not well be contended that the framers of the Constitution *assumed* that the courts would exercise such supervisory power over legislation as they now lay claim to. The debates in the Convention negative any such idea as does the fact that the attempt to exercise such power by the State courts over

[12] *Id.*, p. 399.

[13] Ware v. Hylton, 3 Dallas, 211.

[14] Art. 6, § 2, Constitution of the United States.

State statutes had been sharply rebuked by the people.[15]

Concerning the exercise of this power by the courts, in an early North Carolina case, Mr. Spaight of that state, afterwards Governor of the State, said:

"I do not pretend to vindicate the law which has been the subject of controversy; it is immaterial what they (the courts) have declared void; it is their usurpation of the authority to do it, that I complain of, as I do most positively deny that they have any such power; nor can they find anything in the Constitution, either directly or impliedly, that will support them, or give them any color of right to exercise that authority. Besides, it would have been absurd, and contrary to the practice of all the world, had the Constitution vested such power in them, as they would have operated as an absolute negative on the proceedings of the Legislature, which no judiciary ought ever to possess, and the State, instead of being governed by the representatives in the general assembly, would be subject to the will of three individuals, who united in their own persons the legislative and judiciary powers, which no monarch in Europe enjoys, and which would be more despotic than the Roman decemvirate, and equally insufferable." [16]

[15] *Spirit of American Government,* by Smith, pp. 88–9; *Conflict over Judicial Powers,* by Haines, pp. 32–3.

[16] Haines, *The Conflict over Judicial Powers,* p. 33. See also, opinion of Justice Gibson of Pennsylvania, in Eakin v. Raub, 12 Seargent and Rawle, p. 33.

The above suggested facts and circumstances, while by no means exhausting the subject, go far to support the conclusion reached by careful students of the question that the exercise by the Courts of power to nullify laws as unconstitutional is simply judicial usurpation.[17]

When it is remembered that only thirty-nine of the sixty-five delegates appointed to the Constitutional Convention signed the Constitution, and that it was only after a protracted struggle that the ratification of the necessary number of States was secured, it is obvious that the Constitution would never have been ratified by the people had they suspected that it gave judges the power now exercised by them.

[17] See Hon. Walter Clark, LL.D., Chief Justice of North Carolina, on "Judicial Supremacy," *The Arena*, Feb., 1908.

CHAPTER III

WHY THE PEOPLE DISTRUST THE COURTS

(B) The Courts having seized the power to declare some statutes invalid, because unconstitutional, have come to declare other statutes invalid merely because the judges disapproved the policy of such legislation.

WHETHER the above charge is fully sustained, is a question concerning which there is a difference of opinion. That it is freely made and commonly believed, is undoubted.[1]

It is not open to dispute that the courts have carried the doctrine of judicial nullification of statutes far beyond the boundaries prescribed by the Judges who first asserted the existence of the power in the courts, to declare statutes unconstitutional.

In the earliest case in which the question was con-

[1] *Spirit of American Government,* by Smith; *American Law Review,* Vol. XXVI, p. 169 (article by Judge Seymour D. Thompson); "The Confusion of Property with Privilege," by Jesse F. Orton in the *Independent* of August 19 and 26, 1909; "Government by Judiciary," L. B. Boudin, *Political Science Quarterly,* Vol. XXVI, Nov. 2, 1911; "Flexibility of Law," *The Outlook,* Dec. 17, 1910, Vol. XCVI, p. 848; "The Judge and the People," *The Outlook,* April 15, 1911, Vol. XCVII, pp. 809–10. Also *Outlook* for Jany. 6, 1912 and *Current Literature* for Sept. and Dec., 1911.

sidered by the Supreme Court, though not there decided, it is said:

"To be obliged to act contrary either to the obvious directions of Congress, or to a Constitutional principle in our judgment equally obvious, excited feelings in us we hope never to experience again." [2]

In another early case in which this question was considered by the Supreme Court, but not decided, Mr. Justice Iredell, always a strong advocate of the power of the judiciary to nullify statutes, had this to say:

"If any act of Congress or of the Legislature of a State violates those Constitutional provisions, it is unquestionably void; though I admit that as the authority to declare it void is of a delicate and awful nature, the court will never resort to that authority, but in a *clear* and *urgent* case. If, on the other hand, the Legislature of the Union shall pass a law within the general scope of their constitutional power, the court cannot pronounce it void merely because it is, in their judgment, contrary to the principles of natural justice. The ideas of natural justice are regulated by no fixed standard; the ablest and purest men have differed upon the subject." [3]

In the same opinion, Mr. Justice Iredell, quoted approvingly from Sir William Blackstone, as follows:

[2] Hayburn's case, 2 Dallas, 412.
[3] Calder v. Bull, 3 Dallas, 385, 398.

"There is no Court that has the power to defeat the intent of the Legislature, when couched in such evident and express words, as to leave no doubt whether it was the intent of the Legislature or no. 1 Bl. Com. 91."

In Marbury v. Madison, where the power of the judiciary to nullify statutes is first formally declared, although it was not necessary to the decision of the case, the principle is recognized that it is only Legislation clearly "repugnant to the Constitution" that can be declared void.[4]

Before the Supreme Court had decided that it had power to declare an Act of Congress void, Mr. Justice Chase, in 1796, said:

"If the Court have such power, I am free to declare that I will never exercise it but in a very clear case."[5]

Mr. Justice Strong said in the Legal Tender Cases, decided in 1870:

"It is incumbent, therefore, upon those who affirm the unconstitutionality of an Act of Congress to show clearly that it is in violation of the provisions of the Constitution."[6]

In the Trade Mark Cases, decided in 1879, Mr. Justice Miller said:

[4] 1 Cranch, 137, p. 176. See also, McCulloch v. Maryland, 4 Wheaton, 316–421.

[5] Hylton v. U. S., 3 Dallas, 171.

[6] 12 Wall, 457, p. 531.

"When this Court is called on in the course of the administration of the law to consider whether an act of Congress, or any other department of the government, is within the constitutional authority of that department, a due respect for the coördinate branch of the government requires that we shall decide that it has transcended its powers only when that is so plain that we cannot avoid the duty." [7]

Mr. Justice Story, in 1838, declared that if a statute admitted of two interpretations, one of which made it constitutional and the other not, it was always the duty of the Court to adopt the interpretation which made the statute constitutional, for he said:

"A presumption never ought to be indulged that Congress meant to exercise or usurp any unconstitutional authority unless that conclusion is forced upon the Court by language altogether unambiguous." [8]

In the Sinking Fund Cases, decided in 1878, Mr. Justice Waite said:

"Every possible presumption is in favor of the validity of a statute, and this continues until the contrary is shown beyond a rational doubt. One branch of the government cannot encroach on the domain of another without danger. The safety of our institutions depends in no small degree on a strict observance of this salutary rule." [9]

[7] 100 U. S. 82, p. 96.
[8] 12 Pet. 72, p. 76.
[9] 99 U. S. 700, p. 718.

As late as 1905, Mr. Justice Harlan, in support of the right of the Legislature of New York to limit the hours of work in bakeries, declared:

"If there be *doubt* as to the validity of the statute, that doubt must therefore be resolved in favor of its validity, and the Courts must keep their hands off, leaving the Legislature to meet the responsibility for unwise legislation."[10]

But, alas, this was the language of a dissenting opinion. The majority of the Court had already entered upon the field of judicial legislation, and a statute wholly beneficent passed by the Legislature of New York, approved by the Governor of the State and upheld by the highest Court of the State was stricken down and destroyed by a majority vote of five to four in the Supreme Court of the United States. Five Justices of the Supreme Court pitted their judgment against that of their four associates, and against the wisdom and intelligence of the Legislature and Governor of the State of New York, and the Courts of New York, and declared that the law in question was unconstitutional. To declare a law unconstitutional and void under these circumstances, the Court must indeed have passed far beyond the point where a *doubt* as to its constitutionality required a decision that it was constitutional.

[10] Lochner v. New York, 198 U. S. 45, 68.

The dissenting opinion of Mr. Justice Holmes, in the same case is illuminating.[11] He said:

"I regret sincerely that I am unable to agree with the judgment in this case, and I think it my duty to express my dissent. This case is decided upon an economic theory which a large part of the country does not entertain. If it were a question whether I agree with that theory (limiting the consecutive hours of labor in bakeries which may be required of an employé), I should desire to study it further and long before making up my mind. But I do not conceive that to be my duty, because I strongly believe that my agreement or disagreement has nothing to do with the right of a majority to embody their opinions in law."

Clearly the learned Justice believed and was in this language charging that the majority of the Court was holding the law unconstitutional because the judges constituting a majority of the Court did not believe in the economic theory formulated by the statute. This is made even clearer a little further along in the opinion of Justice Holmes, where he says:

"Some of these laws (referring to those he has just discussed) embody convictions or prejudices which judges are likely to share. Some may not, but a Constitution is not intended to embody a particular economic theory, whether of paternalism and the organic

[11] Lochner v. N. Y., 198 U. S., p. 75.

relation of the citizen to the State, or of *laissez faire.* It is made for people of fundamentally differing views, and the accident of our finding certain opinions natural and familiar or novel, and even shocking, *ought not* to conclude our judgment upon the question whether statutes embodying them conflict with the Constitution of the United States."

This is in effect a frank declaration from a member of the Supreme Court, that in the case under consideration, the statute was held unconstitutional because legislation shortening the hours of labor in the occupation in question, was novel or possibly shocking to the judges constituting the majority of the Court. Note also the provision of the Constitution of the United States which the majority of the Court held was violated by the labor legislation in question. It was the Fourteenth Amendment of the Federal Constitution which it was said forbade such legislation, and the portion thereof which provides:

"No State shall make or enforce any law which shall abridge the privileges or immunities of citizens of the United States; nor shall any State deprive any person of life, liberty or property without due process of law, nor deny to any person within its jurisdiction, the equal protection of the laws."

Every one knows that the sole intent and purpose of the people in adding this amendment to the Constitution, was to protect the then recently emancipated negroes in their rights of citizenship. The courts, however, have made this amendment include all manner of trusts and corporations, and of contracts and practices, none of which were even in the thought of the people when they adopted the amendment. In the hands of the courts, this amendment has become a shield to protect corporations and combinations of wealth from the legislation aimed at them by an indignant public, and also a sword by which statute after statute has been cut down, enacted by the law-making branch of the government in the public interest. No one supposes that even with the public feeling following the Civil War, existing in 1868, when this amendment was adopted, that it would have been accepted by the people, had they even suspected the use that would be made of it. How long the public will continue to submit to this obvious and confessed misapplication of this provision of the Constitution is a question. It is a very foolish person, however, who believes or even hopes that it will do so much longer.

The number of statutes nullified by the courts is large, but the character of much of the legislation thus destroyed is more significant than the volume. In 131 U. S., appendix CCXXXV, a list of statutes is given, both Federal and State, held unconstitutional by the Supreme Court of the United States up to about the year 1887. This list shows that up to the year mentioned, twenty Federal Statutes and one hundred and eighty-five State Statutes were held invalid by the Supreme Court of the United States alone. It is since the above compilation was made, however, that the greater number and most objectionable decisions have been rendered declaring statutes unconstitutional. These decisions have usually been made by a divided Court, and in some cases, the change of a single vote would have completely changed the result. The Legislation thus destroyed was practically all carefully devised to meet existing and recognized evils, and enacted in response to an overwhelming demand of the people.

One of the subjects uppermost in the minds of the people and vitally affecting the life of the Nation is the regulation by statute of the charges of the great public service corporations of the country. This is not the place to dwell upon the necessity for such legislation, nor upon the ability and patriotism of the men engaged in devising it. No more important question was ever presented to our people for solution and no abler men have ever lived in this country, than those who, for the last decade have been trying to bring these vast aggregations of wealth and power under some degree of control. Yet the whole body of law on the subject, built up with such care, has been made a scrap heap of broken and twisted statutes by the decisions of the Federal Courts.[12]

[12] Ex Parte Young, 209 U. S. 123 (1908), sustaining the action of the lower court in punishing a state officer, the

That the railroads and other public service corporations have, in many instances, yielded voluntary obedience to the statutes regulating their rates and charges, more strict than some of those declared unconstitutional by the courts, shows a wholesome respect for the popular will, but does not alter the

attorney-general of Minnesota, for contempt by reason of his official acts performed in obedience to the statute of the State regulating the rates of public service corporations, such action of the attorney-general being contrary to the order of an inferior federal court purporting to restrain the attorney-general from enforcing the statute of his State. (Dissenting opinion by Justice Harlan.)

Galveston, Harrisburg & San Antonio Railway Co. v. State of Texas, 210 U. S. 217 (1908), holding a state statute providing for a percentage tax on the gross receipts of railroad companies within the State unconstitutional and void. (Dissenting opinion by Mr. Justice Harlan with whom concurred Chief Justice Fuller and Mr. Justice White and Mr. Justice McKenna.)

Western Union Telegraph Co. v. State of Kansas, 216 U. S. 1 (1909), holding a statute of Kansas void providing that before a foreign corporation should have authority to do business in the State, it should pay to the State treasurer for the benefit of the school fund, a fee of one-tenth of one per cent. upon the first hundred thousand dollars of its capital stock, and a smaller percentage upon stock in excess of the amount. (Dissenting opinion by Mr. Justice Holmes with whom concurred the Chief Justice and Mr. Justice McKenna.)

Pullman Co. v. Kansas, 216 U. S. 56 (1909), dissents as above. Also opinion in David C. Shepard v. Northern Pacific Railway Co., et al, Sanborn, circuit judge, under date of April 8, 1911, which practically destroyed the Minnesota statute providing for the regulation of rates of public service corporations.

fact that the decisions mentioned, and others like them, if they are accepted as final, leave the great corporations the real masters of the field. The rule of the Minnesota case (Shepard v. Northern Pacific Railway, cited in the note) to the effect practically that a railroad is entitled to a *net income* of seven per cent. on the value of its properties, in each State, such value to be fixed according to a Referee's estimate, necessarily based principally upon figures furnished by the railroad, leaves very little of rate making to be regulated by statute, and seriously cripples the taxing power of the State as well. The finding of the Referee in this case that the reduction of rates complained of must result, either in unjust discrimination in favor of the Minnesota cities, and against those in other States just over the border, or in such readjustment of Interstate rates as constituted an interference with Interstate Commerce can be made and sustained in practically every case where any reduction of rates is ordered by law. By this rule, a State's power to make any general reduction in rates is practically destroyed. This case in principle, at least, I believe is in conflict with the general rule of State courts.[13]

Scarcely second in importance to the regulation

[13] Independent Tug Line v. Lake Superior Lumber Co., 131 N. W. 409 (Wisconsin supreme court, May, 1911; see also, proceedings of governors' conference respecting this case referred to in Chapter I).

of the rates and charges of railways, telegraphs, telephones, sleeping cars and express companies, is that of holding them and other corporations and concerns to a proper rule of accountability for injuries received by their employés in the course of their employment. The hardships of the ancient rules of the common law, holding that employés must assume the risks of their employment, and that employers sustain no liability for damage resulting from the injury or death of an employé, where his own negligence, however slight, or the negligence of another employé caused or contributed to the accident, are too well recognized to require comment. Bad as these rules were when applied in the rude times wherein they originated, to the simple machinery and obvious dangers connected therewith, they have become intolerable as applied by our courts to the dangerous, complicated and complex conditions under which millions of men, women and children in this country are obliged to work. To meet this situation, Congress finally, after much consideration, both by the executive and legislative departments of the government,[14] in 1906 passed, and the President approved, what was know as the "Employers' Liability Act." This act related to the liability of common carriers in the District of Columbia, in the

[14] See President's Annual Message, Dec. 6, 1904, 39 Cong. Rec. 11; of Dec. 5, 1905, 40 Cong. Rec. 93.

Territories, and to common carriers engaged in Interstate Commerce and made such common carriers, while so engaged, liable for all damages resulting from the negligence of its officers, agents or employés, or by reason of any defects resulting from negligence in its cars, machinery, road-bed, etc., and also provided that contributory negligence of an employé should not bar recovery where his negligence was slight, and that of the employer gross, but that damages should be diminished by the Jury in proportion to the amount of negligence attributable to the employé. This statute, the Supreme Court of the United States, by a vote of five to four, held unconstitutional.[15]

Mr. Justice Moody dissented in one of the ablest opinions ever written, and Mr. Justice Harlan, with whom concurred Mr. Justice McKenna, dissented, as did also Mr. Justice Holmes. The opinion of the majority of the Court proceeds upon the idea that the statute in question, while it embraced subjects which Congress had authority to regulate, also included subjects not within the power of Congress to regulate, and therefore held the statute void, and no recovery was allowed to the particular plaintiffs, although as I understand it, it was admitted that the employment in which they were engaged at the time

15 Employers' Liability Cases, 207 U. S. 463, dissenting opinions 504, 541.

of the injury was within the authority of Congress to regulate.[16]

In opening his dissenting opinion, Mr. Justice Moody, said:

"I am unable to agree to the judgment of the court. Under ordinary circumstances, where the judgment rests exclusively, as it does here, upon a mere interpretation of the words of a law, which may be readily changed by the law-making branches of the government, if they be so minded, a difference of opinion may well be left without expression. But where the judgment is a judicial condemnation of an act of a coördinate branch of our government it is so grave a step that no member of the court can escape his own responsibility, or be justified in suppressing his own views, if unhappily they have not found expression in those of his associates. Moved by this consideration, and solicitous to maintain what seem to me the lawful powers of the Nation, I have no doubt of my duty to disclose fully the opinions which, to my regret, differ in some respects from those of some of my brethren."

Can it be that there was not even a "rational doubt" of the constitutionality of this statute, when the four great judges, Harlan, Moody, Holmes and

[16] Docket titles are Damsell Howard, Administratrix of Will Howard, deceased, v. Illinois Cent. R. R. Co. and the Yazoo and Mississippi Valley R. R. Co.; N. C. Brooks, Administratrix of Morris S. Brooks, deceased, v. Southern Pacific Co.

McKenna asserted, in the most vigorous manner, and with all their wealth of learning, that the statute and the Constitution were in perfect harmony, and not in any respect conflicting? Can it be that because the statute contained opinions concerning the relations between employers and employés "novel and even shocking" to some members of the Court, that the judgment of the majority of the Court was thereby influenced or determined?

That Congress was finally able to pass a law relating to the liability of employers engaged in interstate commerce, which met the approval of the Court (Mondou v. N. Y., etc., Ry. Co., U. S. Sup. Ct., Jan. 15, 1912), is not material to the present discussion, except as it may indicate a changed attitude of the Court in deciding whether a statute is constitutional or not.

Shortly after the decision destroying the "Employers' Liability Act," the Supreme Court of the United States also struck down the compulsory arbitration law, reversing by a divided Court the most able decision of the Lower Court, holding the law constitutional.[17] This law was passed as the result of the great railroad strike at Chicago in 1894, and was intended to prevent such unfortunate occurrence in the future by providing for the arbitration of differences between corporations engaged in interstate commerce and their employés, and pro-

[17] Adair v. U. S., 208 U. S. 161, 152 Fed. Rep. 737.

hibiting the discharge of the employés merely because they belonged to Labor Unions. (See p. 164, Adair v. U. S. 208 U. S.) Justices McKenna and Holmes dissented and Mr. Justice Moody took no part in the decision of the case.

State courts of last resort have not always been more kind to statutory changes in the common law, relating to employer and employé than the Federal courts, and in March, 1911, the Court of Appeals of New York, in an elaborate opinion held the workingmen's compensation law of that State unconstitutional, although the lower courts had found no reason to doubt its constitutionality.[18]

Workmen's Compensation laws, during the year 1911, were passed in the States of California, Illinois, Kansas, Massachusetts, Nevada, New Jersey, Ohio, Vermont, and Wisconsin. These laws are all of the same general character, and are permissive, or optional; that is, they leave it to the employer and employé to determine whether the provisions of the law will be accepted or not. But as an inducement to employers to accept the terms of the law, it is

[18] Ives v. South Buffalo Railway Co., 201 N. Y. 271, reversing 140 App. Div. 921. The correctness of the decision in the Ives case is denied by the Supreme Court of Washington, in a decision handed down September 27, 1911, upholding the Workmen's Compensation Law of that state, which differs in no substantial particular as to the constitutional question involved from the law which the New York Court of Appeals declared unconstitutional. State v. Clausen, 117 Pac. Rep. 1101.

uniformly provided, that the defenses of "assumed risk" and the "fellow servant rule" are abolished, and in some cases the defense of contributory negligence much limited. If the employer does not choose to accept the privileges of the law, he loses the above defenses when sued by the employé in a common law action. The administration of the law is placed in the hands of a board or commission. These laws provide a comprehensive scheme by which, after the parties have elected to accept the provisions thereof, any substantial injury received by the employé in the course of or incidental to his employment, except those caused by his own wilful misconduct, shall be compensated for by the employer, according to certain definite rules which are to be administered by the board or commission above mentioned. The rules of procedure are definitely laid down; both parties are given notice of hearings; the amount to be paid in case of death and in case of certain described injuries, is provided for. The whole proceeding is simple, expeditious and inexpensive. The opinion of the Wisconsin Supreme Court, rendered November 14th, 1911 (133 Northwestern Reporter, 209), upholding the law in that State, is elaborate, and constitutes a most valuable contribution to the subject.

In the main opinion rendered by Winslow, C. J., it is said:

"It is matter of common knowledge that this law forms the legislative response to an emphatic, if not a peremptory, public demand. It was admitted by lawyers, as well as laymen, that the personal injury action brought by the employé against his employer to recover damages for injuries sustained by reason of the negligence of the employer had wholly failed to meet or remedy a great economic and social problem which modern industrialism has forced upon us, namely, the problem of who shall make pecuniary recompense for the toll of suffering and death which that industrialism levies and must continue to levy upon the civilized world. This problem is distinctly a modern problem. In the days of manual labor, the small shop, with few employés, and the stage coach, there was no such problem, or, if there was, it was almost negligible. Accidents there were in those days, and distressing ones; but they were relatively few, and the employé who exercised any reasonable degree of care was comparatively secure from injury. There was no army of injured and dying, with constantly swelling ranks marching with halting step and dimming eyes to the great hereafter. This is what we have with us now, thanks to the wonderful material progress of our age, and this is what we shall have with us for many a day to come. Legislate as we may in the line of stringent requirements for safety devices or the abolition of employers' common-law defenses, the army of the injured will still increase, and the price of our manufacturing greatness will still have to be paid in human blood and tears. To speak of the common-law personal injury action as a remedy for this problem is to jest with serious subjects, to give a stone to one who asks for bread. The terrible economic waste, the overwhelming temptation to the commission of perjury, and the relatively small proportion of the sums recovered which comes to the injured parties in such actions, condemn them as wholly inadequate to meet the difficulty.

"In approaching the consideration of the present law, we must bear in mind the well-established principle that it must be sustained, unless it *be clear beyond reasonable question* that it violates some constitutional limitation or prohibition. . . . A constitution is a very human document, and must embody with greater or less fidelity the spirit of the time of its adoption. It will be framed to meet the problems and difficulties which face the men who make it, and it will generally crystallize with more or less fidelity the political, social, and economic propositions which are considered irrefutable, if not actually inspired, by the philosophers and legislators of the time; but the difficulty is that, while the Constitution is fixed or very hard to change, the conditions and problems surrounding the people, as well as their ideals, are constantly changing. The political or philosophical aphorism of one generation is doubted by the next, and entirely discarded by the third. The race moves forward constantly, and no Canute can stay its progress.

"Constitutional commands and prohibitions, either distinctly laid down in express words or necessarily implied from general words, must be obeyed, and implicitly obeyed, so long as they remain unamended or unrepealed. Any other course on the part of either legislator or judge constitutes violation of his oath of office; but when there is no such express command or prohibition, but only general language, or a general policy drawn from the four corners of the instrument, what shall be said about this? By what standards is this general language or general policy to be interpreted and applied to present day people and conditions? When an eighteenth century constitution forms the charter of liberty of a twentieth century government, must its general provisions be construed and interpreted by an eighteenth century mind in the light of eighteenth century conditions and ideals? Clearly not. This were to command the race to halt in its progress, to stretch the state upon a veritable bed of Procrustes."

I close what I have to say on this particular point with a reference to the well-known income tax cases wherein, by the change in the vote of a single member of the Supreme Court of the United States, the government was deprived of the power conceded to it for a hundred years, to raise revenue by a tax upon the large incomes of the rich.[19]

While the facts of these cases are generally well understood, it is perhaps not amiss to restate them here.

In August, 1894, Congress passed a statute (28 Stat. 509 c. 349) which provided in substance for a tax of two per centum on net incomes above four thousand dollars. Shortly after the passage of the

[19] Pollock v. Farmers' Loan & Trust Co., 157 U. S. 429, 654; Pollock v. Farmers' Loan & Trust Co. (re-hearing), 158 U. S. 601, 715.

act, Charles Pollock, a citizen of Massachusetts, brought an action in the Federal Court, alleging that he was a stockholder in the Farmers' Loan & Trust Company, a corporation, of the State of New York, and that said company was about to pay the tax above mentioned, as required by the statute, and prayed that the payment of the tax be enjoined. It is obvious from the record that the controversy presented was not a real one, but that the action was brought with the approval of the defendant, and for the purpose merely of procuring a decision on the constitutionality of the law.

At the time of the first argument in the Supreme Court, which occurred in March, 1895, Mr. Justice Jackson was ill and took no part in the case. The remainder of the Court, consisting of eight members, was equally divided on all questions concerning the constitutionality of the act except the provision imposing a tax upon rents and incomes from real estate. As the Lower Court had sustained the constitutionality of the act, the effect of this decision was to uphold the law, except as to the single item of rents and incomes from real estate, and in respect to this tax, the court, by a bare majority [20] held it unconstitutional.

At the re-argument, Mr. Justice Jackson had so

[20] See conclusion of Chief Justice Fuller's opinion, 157 U. S., p. 586, and beginning of dissenting opinion of Mr. Justice Harlan, 158 U. S. 638.

far recovered his health, as to participate therein, and wrote vigorously in behalf of sustaining the law, as did also Justices Harlan, Brown and White. One of the judges, however, who had previously voted to sustain the law, changed his vote and while the record of the cases contains no word from this Justice explaining the reasons for his action, the result was the total annihilation of the law.

The considerations which influenced the views of the majority of the Court are well stated by Mr. Justice Field in his opinion, where he said: [21]

> "The present assault upon capital is but the beginning. It will be but the stepping stone to others, larger and more sweeping, till our political contests will become a war of the poor against the rich; a war constantly growing in intensity and bitterness.— If the purely arbitrary limitation of four thousand dollars in the present law can be sustained, none having less than that amount of income being assessed, or taxed for the support of the government, the limitation of future Congresses may be fixed at a much larger sum, at five or ten or twenty thousand dollars, parties possessing an income of that amount alone being bound to bear the burdens of government; or the limitation may be designated at such an amount as a Board of 'Walking Delegates' may deem necessary."

Was it because the majority of the Court regarded this law as contrary to some clause of the Constitu-

[21] 157 U. S., p. 607.

tion or because they regarded it as an "assault upon capital" that they destroyed it?

Mr. Justice Jackson said:[22]

"The decision (of the majority of the court) disregards the well established canon of construction to which I have referred that an act passed by a coördinate branch of the government has every presumption in its favor, and should never be declared invalid by the courts unless its repugnancy to the Constitution is clear beyond all reasonable doubt. It is not a matter of conjecture; it is the established principle that it must be clear beyond a reasonable doubt. I cannot see, in view of the past, how this case can be said to be free of doubt. Again, the decision not only takes from Congress its rightful power of fixing the rate of taxation, but substitutes a rule incapable of application without producing the most monstrous inequality and injustice between citizens residing in different sections of their common country, such as the framers of the Constitution never could have contemplated, such as no free and enlightened people can ever possibly sanction or approve. The practical operation of the decision is not only to disregard the great principles of equality in taxation, but the further principle that in the imposition of taxes for the benefit of the government, the burdens thereof should be imposed upon those having most *ability* to bear them. This decision in effect works out a directly opposite result in relieving the citizens having the greater *ability*, while the burdens of taxation are

22 158 U. S., p. 705.

made to fall most heavily and oppressively upon those having the least ability. . . . Considered in all its bearings, this decision is, in my judgment, the most disastrous blow ever struck at the Constitutional power of Congress."

Mr. Justice Brown said:[23]

"While I have no doubt that Congress will find some means of surmounting the present crisis, my fear is that in some moment of national peril, this decision will rise up to frustrate its will and paralyze its arm. I hope it may not prove the first step toward the despotism of wealth. As I cannot escape the conviction that the decision of the court in this great case is fraught with immeasurable danger to the future of the country, and that it approaches the proportions of a national calamity, I feel it a duty to enter my protest against it."

Mr. Justice Harlan said:[24]

"It nevertheless results that those parts of the (*Wilson*) act that survive the new theory of the Constitution evolved by these cases, are those imposing burdens upon the great body of the American people who derive no rents from real estate, and who are not so fortunate as to own invested personal property, such as the bonds or stocks of corporations, that hold within their control almost the entire business of the country. Such a result is one to be deeply deplored. It cannot be regarded otherwise than as a disaster to the country.

[23] 158 U. S., p. 695. [24] *Id.*, pp. 684–5.

The decree now passed dislocates — principally, for reasons of an economic nature — a sovereign power expressly granted to the general government and long recognized and fully established by judicial decisions and legislative actions. It so interprets constitutional provisions, originally designed to protect the slave property against oppressive taxation, as to give privileges and immunities never contemplated by the founders of the government. . . . The serious aspect of the present decision is that by a new interpretation of the Constitution, it so ties the hands of the legislative branch of the government, that without an amendment of that instrument, or unless this court, at some future time, should return to the old theory of the Constitution, Congress cannot subject to taxation — however great the needs or pressing the necessities of the government — either the invested personal property of the country, bonds, stocks and investments of all kinds, or the income arising from the renting of real estate, or from the yield of personal property, except by a grossly unequal and unjust rule of apportionment among the States. Thus, undue and disproportioned burdens are placed upon the many, while the few . . . are permitted to evade their share of responsibility for the support of the government ordained for the protection of the rights of all. I cannot assent to an interpretation of the Constitution that impairs and cripples the just powers of the National government in the essential matter of taxation, and at the same time discriminates against the greater part of the people of our country."

Since this case was decided, seventeen years ago, the people, with remarkable but ever diminishing patience, have been seeking to so amend their Constitution as to escape the injustice thrust upon them by the five men constituting the majority of the Supreme Court, when the Income Tax cases were decided. Virtually the change of the vote of one man, as we have seen, changed the result. The Hon. Walter Clark, Chief Justice of the Supreme Court of North Carolina, discussing this decision in 1906 said:[25]

"One man nullified the action of Congress and the President and seventy-five millions of living people and in thirteen years since has taxed the property and labor of the country by his sole vote, one billion, three million dollars, which Congress in compliance with the public will, and relying upon previous decisions of the court, had decreed should be paid out of the excessive incomes of the rich."

Whether we agree with the views of the majority or minority of the Supreme Court in these cases, or with the member of it who voted on both sides of the question, the quotations above set forth show that the question really in the minds of the judges was the expediency or propriety of the income tax law, and not whether it conflicted with any part of

[25] Address before Law Department of University of Pennsylvania in 1906, printed in pamphlet form.

the Constitution. Since members of the Supreme Court have declared that not only the income tax law, but the other great statutes considered above were held invalid, not because they were plainly in conflict with the Constitution, but because they embody economic theories to which a majority of the court were opposed, we may fairly accept as settled the proposition that the courts do invalidate statutes merely because they disapprove the policy embodied in such statutes.

CHAPTER IV

WHY THE PEOPLE DISTRUST THE COURTS

(C) By reading their own view into statutes to the exclusion of the Legislative intention, the members of the judiciary, in effect, become the law-making branch of the Government.

CLOSELY allied to the subject last discussed is the charge that the courts, having learned to destroy statutes of which they disapproved, by holding them to be unconstitutional, have come to interpret statutes admittedly constitutional, so as to make them express the views of the judges constituting the Court, even if thereby they disregard the intention of the law-making branch of the government.

That this charge rests upon a substantial basis of fact is well known to every practicing lawyer. Every lawyer of large experience, can readily add from his own practice and observation, many cases, to the few I shall cite, in proof of the charge here considered. Indeed, it is rather to point out the evils that result from this practice of the courts than to prove its existence that I discuss the subject at all.

While the framers of our Constitution and the

founders of this government disagreed upon many things, they were all agreed, from Hamilton, representing one extreme thought, to Jefferson, representing the other, that the legislative and judicial branches of the government must be kept separate. It is the essence of tyranny to combine in one individual, power to make laws and also power to determine their meaning and application. Under such a system, general rules of law, which all must obey would cease to exist, and we would have what Mr. Justice Lurton of the United States Supreme Court recently declared to be "A Government of Men" instead of "A Government of Law."[1] It is true, the learned Justice says that he sees nothing in the history of the judiciary which "supports an expectation that the function of interpreting will be tortured into an exercise of legislative power." He further says:

> "The rules of construction are plain and simple of application. They are in substance identical, whether the instrument for interpretation be a statute or a contract."[2]

Judge Lurton, however, agrees that nothing but disaster could result from the exercise by the Judiciary of any sort of legislative power. Bad as

[1] *North American Review*, Vol. CXCIII, p. 24.

[2] "A Government of Law or a Government of Men," by Mr. Justice Lurton, Jan., 1911, issue of *North American Review*, Vol. CXCIII, p. 24.

all admit it would be to combine in one person legislative and judicial power, when done constitutionally or in a lawful manner, it is infinitely worse if legislative power is in fact exercised by the Judiciary, but without any right so to do. In such case, to the baneful results that must always follow the exercise of legislative power by a judicial officer, are added those that ever accompany the offense of usurpation; and the people will soon come to distrust the motive of the Court, where otherwise they would only condemn its act.

Mr. Justice Lurton in the paragraph quoted above from his article in the *North American Review* refers to "the rules of construction" which the courts apply in the interpretation of statutes as "plain and simple of application." If the courts refuse to give effect to the intention of the law-making branch of the government, as expressed in a statute, it does not help the case to say that this was done according to "rules of Construction." For example, it is a familiar rule of construction that the courts will not give effect to a statute changing the common law unless the legislative intention is expressed in "unmistakable terms." As there is a great body of statute law, the purpose of which is to change the hardships, injustice and cruelties of the common law, the result is that under cover of this rule, much of this beneficent legislation has failed of its purpose, for it is practically impossible to frame a statute, so that its meaning is "unmistakable" to one who has no sympathy with its purpose. A few illustrations will serve to make this clearer than any amount of discussion.

A few years ago, Congress passed for the District of Columbia, a law relieving married women from their common law disabilities. The statute, among other things provided:

> "Married women shall have power to engage in any business and to contract, whether engaged in business or not, and to sue separately upon their contracts, and also to sue separately for the recovery, security or protection of their property, and for torts committed against them as fully and freely as if they were unmarried."

A man having committed a particularly brutal assault upon his wife (whether they were living together or not does not appear), she brought an action against him to recover damages for the assault. Her right to maintain such an action was rested upon the provisions of the statute above quoted which gave to married women the right to recover for an assault committed upon them as fully and freely as if they were unmarried. When the case finally reached the Supreme Court of the United States, however, as it did in 1910, that Court decided by a majority vote that the statute gave plaintiff no right of action.[3] The majority opinion refers to the fact that at com-

[3] Thompson v. Thompson, 218 U. S. 611.

mon law, the wife could not maintain an action against her husband nor indeed maintain any action, unless she joined her husband, and that her identity in law was practically merged in his. It is then said:

"It may be presumed that the Legislators who enacted this statute were familiar with the long established policy of the common law and were not unmindful of the radical changes in the policy of centuries, which such legislation, as is here suggested, would bring about. Conceding it to be within the power of the legislature to make this alteration in the law if it saw fit to do so, nevertheless such radical and far-reaching changes should only be wrought by language so clear and plain as to be *unmistakable* evidence of the legislative intention."

Mr. Justice Harlan, with whom concurred Justices Holmes and Hughes, dissented. Mr. Justice Harlan, in his dissenting opinion, referring to this statutory provision, said:

"In my opinion, these statutory provisions, properly construed, embrace such a case as the present one. If the words used by Congress lead to such a result, and if, as suggested, that result be undesirable on grounds of public policy, it is not within the functions of the Court to ward off the dangers feared or the evils threatened simply by judicial construction that will defeat the plainly expressed will of the legislative department. With the mere policy, expediency, or justice of legislation, the Courts, in our system of government, have no *rightful* concern. Their duty is only to declare what the law is, not what, in their judgment, it ought to be —leaving the responsibility for legislation where it exclusively belongs, that is with the legislative department, so long as it keeps within Constitutional limits. Now, there is not here, as I think, any room whatever for mere construction,—so explicit are the words of Congress."

Again referring to the decision of the majority of the Court, he says:

"The judgment just rendered will have, as I think, the effect to defeat the clearly expressed will of the Legislature by a construction of its words that cannot be reconciled with their ordinary meaning."

It is true that of the seven members constituting the Court when this decision was rendered, Mr. Justice Lurton stood with the majority but it will appear, I think, to the mind not fearful of the "radical changes in the policy of centuries" which this statute brought about, that the minority and not the majority of the Court followed the "plain and simple" rules of construction. The logical result of this decision must be to deny the wife the right to sue the husband on contract, as well as in tort, and thus leave her where she was at common law, so far as any injury to her personal or property rights by her husband is concerned.

In the note, I give a few out of hundreds of decisions that might be cited illustrating how difficult the courts have made it to change by statute the common law rules applicable to employer and employé in such manner as to give the latter substantial rights against the former which he did not possess at common law.[4]

Two recent decisions of the New York Court of Appeals well illustrate the subject under consideration. One of the abuses from which the people of New York City suffered for a long time was the refusal of the various corporations owning or operating street railroads therein to give transfers to passengers from one line to another. While by a system of leases and contracts the street railroads were under one management and for all practical purposes, were one con-

[4] Gombert v. McKay, 201 N. Y. 27 (decided Feb. 7, 1911), holding that because the section of the New York labor law there considered did not in terms deny to the employer the defenses of assumed risk and contributory negligence that such defenses were available and plaintiff could not recover; Ives v. South Buffalo Railway Co., 201 N. Y. 272 (decided March 24, 1911), holding that because the section of the New York labor law there in question did in terms make the employer liable without regard to negligence and assumption of risk, the statute was unconstitutional and the plaintiff could not recover; Kellogg v. New York Edison Co., 120 App. Div. 410 (N. Y.); Milligan v. Clayville Knitting Co., 137 App. Div. 383 (N. Y.); Heiser v. Cincinnati, etc., Co., 141 A. D. (N. Y.) 400; McGowan v. New York Contracting Co., 143 A. D. (N. Y.) 1; Kimmerle v. Carey Printing Co., 144 A. D. (N. Y.) 714.

cern, yet as sections of the roads were owned by separate corporations, separate fares were extorted from passengers where they passed from one line to the other, even on continuous trips. To meet this abuse, a few years ago, the Legislature of New York passed a law requiring transfers to be given to any passenger making a continuous trip over the roads covered by the lease or contract, so as to entitle the passenger to a continuous passage over the line in question for the single fare of five cents. The purpose of the statute was declared to be that

> "public convenience may be promoted by the operation of the railroads embraced in such contract substantially as a single railroad with a single rate of fare."[5]

In order to secure the enforcement of this law, the Legislature further provided:

> "For every refusal to comply with the requirement of this section, the corporation so refusing shall forfeit fifty dollars to the aggrieved party. The provisions of this section shall only apply to railroads wholly within the limits of any one incorporated city or village."[6]

The street railroads, having refused to give the transfers required by law, actions were brought to recover the penalty of fifty dollars for each refusal

[5] Sec. 104, N. Y. Railroad Law.
[6] Sec. 104, N. Y. Railroad Law.

so to do. One action was brought by Mr. Scudder, a Minister of the Gospel, to recover two hundred and fifty dollars, or five penalties of fifty dollars each, for the refusal of the street railroad company on five separate occasions to give him transfers required by law. Mr. Scudder recovered in the lower Court.[7]

Mr. Griffin, a piano dealer, likewise brought an action to recover four penalties for the refusal of the street railway company, on four separate occasions, to give him transfers as required by law in trips to and from his place of business. He recovered in the lower Court.[8]

These cases were appealed by the street railway company to the New York Court of Appeals and the decision there is referred to as the Griffin case.[9]

The Court of Appeals, after holding that the law had been violated by defendant in refusing transfers, arrived at the conclusion that but one penalty could be recovered. The process of reasoning by which this conclusion is reached is thus stated in the opinion of the Court:[10]

"Referring once more to the language of Section 104 of the Railroad Law, imposing a penalty, we find the single sentence in which it is contained, opening with the words 'for every refusal to comply.' It is quite

7 Scudder v. Interurban Street Railway Co., 96 A. D. 340.

8 Griffin v. Interurban Street Railway Co., 96 A. D. 636.

9 179 N. Y. 438.

10 179 N. Y. 449.

obvious that the legislative intention to permit the recovery of cumulative penalties for refusals of the defendant to comply with the provisions of the railroad law in regard to the transfer of passengers, is as clearly manifested as in any of the cases cited. Notwithstanding this fact, a majority of my brethren are of the opinion that while the rule for the recovery of cumulative penalties, as already adverted to, is firmly established by the earlier decisions of this Court, yet the changed conditions in the modern life of great cities render its modification imperative. . . . The Court is of the opinion that if cumulative recoveries are to be permitted, the Legislature should state its intention in so many words; that a more definite form of statement be substituted for the words *hitherto* deemed sufficient. . . . A sound public policy requires that only one penalty should be recovered in a single action, and that the institution of an action for a penalty is to be regarded as a waiver of all previous penalties incurred."

The effect of this decision was, of course, to operate as a practical repeal of the statute, since the cost to the plaintiff of suing for a single penalty would be more than the amount he could hope to recover. While this decision did not call forth a dissenting opinion in the Court of Appeals, Mr. Justice Gaynor, while a member of the Appellate Division of the Supreme Court (which is inferior to the Court of Appeals), declined to follow the rule it laid down and stated his reasons thus:

"The statute in express terms provides that 'For every refusal to comply with the requirements of this section, the corporation so refusing shall forfeit fifty dollars to the aggrieved party.' We have no right to nullify this statute by holding that the bringing of each successive action for a penalty waives all penalties incurred prior to the bringing of such action, and the actions brought therefor. The Legislature has declared no such thing, but the very contrary. A court of last resort may disregard legislation, or even legislate, *but only because there is no superior authority to reverse its action.* This court is not in that position. It is for it to follow the statutes, and leave it to the highest court to dispense with their operation, if that course is to be pursued. We can declare no 'sound public policy' as against a statute, and substitute it for the statute. Public policy must be looked for in our statutes, in so far as they have spoken, not outside of them. And I venture to say that there is no public policy for the shielding of railroad companies from the payment of statute penalties which they persistently incur year after year, but the contrary. For street railroad companies to continuously refuse for many years — for ten years — to give the transfers over their connecting lines required by statute is a condition of things 'in the modern life of great cities' which public policy requires should be visited with all the prescribed penalties, instead of being shielded from them by the courts against the expressed will of the Legislature. . . . The Legislature followed a line of decisions of the Court of Appeals, cited in the Griffin case, in using the phrase 'every refusal' in the Railroad Law. It is now told that its language is not plain enough. I hope I may say with the highest respect for all concerned that I do not see how the Legislature can make its meaning plainer without passing a bill of remonstrance that it means just what it says." [11]

Mr. Justice Gaynor, since the foregoing dissenting opinion was delivered, was elected Mayor of Greater New York.

To get the full force of the decision of the Court of Appeals in the above case, it should be contrasted with another and later decision of the same Court.[12] The statute under consideration in this case related to the adulteration of foods and provided:

> "Every person violating the provisions of this article shall forfeit and pay to the people of the State the sum of one hundred dollars for each violation."

Special agents of the government, having bought from a dealer, fifteen samples of vinegar, which it was claimed violated the law, an action was brought to recover the aggregate penalties. The defendant naturally defended on the theory that within the rule of the Griffin case, above noticed, it was liable at most for only one penalty. The Court of Appeals,

[11] Harkow v. New York City Railway Co., 121 A. D. 194, p. 196.

[12] People v. Spencer, 201 N. Y. 105. (Decided Feb. 14, 1911.)

however, construed this statute to mean that a separate recovery could be had for each violation, and in order to distinguish the Griffin case, said:

> "Cumulative recoveries will not be permitted by the courts in the absence of such a definite statement by the Legislature, as to leave its intention in that respect *unmistakable.* When that appears, effect will be given to the Legislative intent."[13]

Put the two statutes above quoted side by side. One of them provides that "for every refusal" to give a transfer, the railroad company shall forfeit fifty dollars to the aggrieved party. The other provides "every person violating the provisions of this article" shall forfeit for each violation one hundred dollars to the State. Now determine whether the Court gave effect to the intention of the Legislature in the street railway cases, or whether it gave effect to its own notion of what the law ought to be.

It is with satisfaction that I now call attention to a case wherein the opinion, misinterpreting a statute, was delivered by the minority instead of the majority of the Court, and therefore did no harm.

Preceding the Republican State Convention in Wisconsin, in 1904, that State was the scene of a conflict which, in its intensity and bitterness, resembled a civil war rather than a political campaign. The issue was state regulation of the rates and charges

[13] People v. Spencer, 201 N. Y. 105, p. 109.

of railways. Unless a law providing for such regulation could be passed, the reform movement of that State, which had started some ten years previously, was, as it seemed, destined to complete failure. The railways and other interests benefiting by special privilege, believed if they could prevent the passage of such a law and halt the reform forces at that point, they would eventually force the repeal of the law taxing railways as other property was taxed, and all the other reform legislation passed during the preceding two years of Governor La Follette's administration.

It is no part of my purpose to describe the memorable campaign which preceded the Republican Convention in that State in 1904. Its record is written large in the history of the Progressive Movement which has taken place in this country during the last fifteen years. Suffice it to say that the Convention, which assembled in Madison, Wisconsin, in June, 1904, renominated Mr. La Follette for a third term as Governor, and a state ticket in sympathy with him, and adopted a platform which rang true on the principles of railway rate regulation. A number of delegates, however, bolted the convention and organized another meeting, which assumed to nominate a Republican Candidate for Governor in opposition to Mr. La Follette. The Secretary of State, having refused to give to the bolting nominee the place on the ballot assigned to nominees of the Republican party, application was made to the Courts of the State to compel the Secretary of State so to do.

The Wisconsin Statute, in force at the time in question, which provided for settling disputes of precisely this character by the State Central Committee, was as follows:

> "When two or more conventions or caucuses shall be held and the nominations thereof certified, each claiming to be the regular convention or caucus of the same political party, preference in designation (on the ballot) shall be given to the nominations of the one certified by the committee which had been officially certified to be authorized to represent the party." [14]

The Committee which had been officially certified to be authorized to represent the party certified the nomination of Mr. La Follette and his associates. Concerning this there was no dispute. Respecting the reasoning of the counsel for plaintiff, who contended that the statute above quoted did not apply, Mr. Justice Marshall, writing for the majority of the court said: [15]

> "To our minds the fundamental infirmity in such reasoning is the assumption that there is ambiguity (in the above quoted statute) when there is none in fact."

[14] Sec. 35, subd. 2, Wisconsin Statutes, State ex rel Cook v. Houser, 122 Wisconsin, 534, p. 562.

[15] 122 Wis., p. 568.

Further, Mr. Justice Marshall said:

"Judicial construction can never legitimately commence, until certainty as to what is the sense intended (in the statute) is found to be so obscure that it might reasonably be said to be one thing or another, either being within the fair scope of the words used to express the purpose."

Mr. Justice Winslow, also writing for the majority of the Court in the same case said:

"The question is whether the Legislature has created a special tribunal for the decision of controversies as to rights upon the official ballot, and this question brings me necessarily to the consideration of Sec. 35, Statutes 1898 (the one above quoted) for this is the only section which can be claimed to have that effect. . . . Is it obscure or of doubtful meaning? I confess that when I first read it I could see no difficulty in construing it, nor have I been able to see any such difficulty since that time. It seemed, and now seems to me to be clear and simple; so clear and simple in fact as not to need construction."

Note now that the venerable Chief Justice of the Court took a view of the statute directly opposite to that of the majority. He said:

"If the rules of construction thus quoted are applicable to the provisions of Sec. 35 in question — and I think they are — and if my conclusion as to the facts of the case presented are correct — and I believe they are — then the second clause of the section (the one quoted above) has no application and the State Central Committee had no jurisdiction to determine the controversy in question."

Had the views of the Chief Justice prevailed in this case, it may well be that the Progressive Movement would have been turned back in Wisconsin and halted in the Nation. It is to be regretted that in the Wisconsin case, the opinion of the Chief Justice favored that faction of the party with which he was in avowed sympathy. It is unfortunate that the construction of the statutes considered in the other cases above referred to, and hundreds like them, results uniformly in favor of those interests which a large proportion of the judges represented while practicing as attorneys. The mass of people understand only the results of the decisions, and with those results they are not satisfied.

Two cases were recently decided by the Supreme Court of the United States, which well illustrate the subject here discussed.[16] I shall close what I have to say on the subject of Judicial Legislation by an examination of these cases. It must be constantly borne in mind that the cases dealt with in this branch of the discussion, are those decided by the most emi-

[16] Standard Oil Company of New Jersey, et al, Appellants, v. United States. Opinion delivered May 15, 1911, 221 U. S. 1; United States v. American Tobacco Company, et al. Opinion delivered May 29, 1911, 221 U. S. 106.

nent courts of last resort in the country, and whatever vices appear in the construction of statute by these courts, *are multiplied many times in the decisions of inferior courts.*

In 1890 Congress passed what is known as the Anti-Trust Act. This act provides:

> "*Every* contract, combination in the form of trust or otherwise, or conspiracy, in restraint of trade or commerce among the several States, or foreign nations, is hereby declared to be illegal."

The entire act, so far as it is material, is given in the margin.[17] The reasons which led to the passage

[17] Sec. 1. *Every* contract, combination in the form of trust or otherwise, or conspiracy, in restraint of trade or commerce among the several states, or with foreign nations, is hereby declared to be illegal. Every person who shall make *any such contract or engage in any such combination or conspiracy,* shall be deemed guilty of a misdemeanor, and on conviction thereof, shall be punished by fine not exceeding $5,000, or by imprisonment not exceeding one year, or by both said punishments in the discretion of the court. Sec. 2. Every person who shall monopolize or attempt to monopolize, or combine or conspire with any other person or persons, to monopolize *any part* of the trade or commerce among the several states, or with foreign nations, shall be deemed guilty of a misdemeanor, and, on conviction thereof, shall be punished by a fine not exceeding $5,000, or by imprisonment not exceeding one year, or by both said punishments, in the discretion of the court. Sec. 3. *Every* contract, combination in form of trust *or otherwise,* or conspiracy, in restraint of trade or commerce in any territory of the United States, or of the District of Columbia, or in restraint of trade or com-

of this Act are undisputed and are set forth by Mr. Justice Harlan, in his opinion in the Standard Oil case, as follows:

"All who recall the condition of the country in 1890 will remember that there was everywhere among the people generally a deep feeling of unrest. The Nation had been rid of human slavery — fortunately, as all now feel — but the conviction was universal that the country was in real danger from another kind of slavery sought to be fastened on the American people, namely, the slavery that would result from aggregations of capital in the hands of a few individuals and corporations controlling, for their own profit and advantage exclusively, the entire business of the country, including the production and sale of the necessaries of life. Such a danger was thought to be imminent, and all felt that it must be met firmly and by such statutory regulations as would adequately protect the people against oppression and wrong."

Of course, Congress could only legislate as to interstate commerce, that is, commerce which in some way involved acts or traffic in more than one State.

merce between any such territory and another, or between any such territory or territories and any state or states or the District of Columbia, or with foreign nations, is hereby declared illegal. Every person who shall make any *such* contract or engage in any *such* combination or conspiracy shall be deemed guilty of a misdemeanor, and, on conviction thereof, shall be punished by fine not exceeding $5,000, or by imprisonment not exceeding one year, or by both said punishments, in the discretion of the court. (26 Stat. 209, c. 657.)

A commercial transaction entirely within a state would be subject to the laws of that State, and not to the laws of the United States. In our country, however, much the larger part of commerce is interstate, so that the regulation of interstate commerce in a large measure, regulates the entire subject.

Shortly after the Anti-Trust Act of 1890 was passed, the United States brought an action to declare void as contrary to the act, a contract, made between a large number of railroads, intended to secure uniform classification of rates and to prevent secret cutting of rates, and for other purposes therein stated. The case finally reached the Supreme Court of the United States in December, 1896, and was decided in March, 1897, and that Court held, five judges to four, that the Act in question was violated by the contract between the railroads, and gave judgment annulling the contract.[18] Mr. Justice White wrote a long and vigorous dissenting opinion, *but he was then in the minority.* The principal contention on the part of the railroads in that case was, and the principal contention in the opinion of Mr. Justice White likewise was, that the statute above quoted should be read as though the word "unreasonable" or "undue" had been inserted before the word "restraint," thus making the statute read:

[18] United States v. Trans-Missouri Freight Association, 166 U. S. 290, 374.

"Every contract, combination in the form of trust or otherwise or conspiracy in *unreasonable* or *undue* restraint of trade or commerce among the several states or foreign nations is hereby declared to be illegal."

After most elaborate arguments, however, the theory of construction which involved interpolating into the statute the word "unreasonable" or its equivalent word "undue" was *rejected*. Mr. Justice Peckham, writing for the majority of the Court said:

"As a result of this review of the situation, we find two very widely divergent views of the effects which might be expected to result from declaring illegal all contracts in restraint of trade, etc.; one side predicting financial disaster and ruin to competing railroads, including thereby the ruin of shareholders, the destruction of immensely valuable properties, and the consequent prejudice to the public interest; while on the other side predictions equally earnest are made that no such mournful results will follow, and it is urged that there is a necessity, in order that the public interest may be fairly and justly protected, to allow free and open competition among railroads upon the subject of the rates for the transportation of persons and property.

"The arguments which have been addressed to us against the inclusion of all contracts in restraint of trade, as provided for by the language of the act, have been based upon the alleged presumption that Congress, notwithstanding the language of the act, could not have intended to embrace all contracts, but only such contracts as were in unreasonable restraint of trade. Under these circumstances we are, therefore, asked to hold that the act of Congress excepts contracts which are not in unreasonable restraint of trade, and which only keep rates up to a reasonable price, notwithstanding the language of the act makes no such exception. In other words, we are asked to read into the act *by way of judicial legislation* an exception that is not placed there by the lawmaking branch of the government, and this is to be done upon the theory that the impolicy of such legislation is so clear that it cannot be supposed Congress intended the natural import of the language it used. This we cannot and ought not to do. That impolicy is not so clear, nor are the reasons for the exception so potent as to permit us to interpolate an exception into the language of the act, and thus materially alter its meaning and effect. It may be that the policy evidenced by the passage of the act itself will, if carried out, result in disaster to the roads and in a failure to secure the advantages sought from such legislation. Whether that will be the result or not we do not know and cannot predict. These considerations are, however, not for us. If the act ought to read as contended for by defendants, Congress is the body to amend it, and not this court, by a process of judicial legislation wholly unjustifiable."

With the above opinion of Mr. Justice Peckham, Chief Justice Fuller, Mr. Justice Harlan, Mr. Justice Brewer and Mr. Justice Brown concurred. It was necessary to the determination of this case, to decide whether the word "unreasonable" could be read into the statute, for it was not found that the contract condemned was in unreasonable restraint of trade. Mr. Justice White makes this very clear in his dissenting opinion. He says: [19]

"The theory upon which the contract is held to be illegal is that even though it be reasonable, and hence valid, under the general principles of law, it is yet void, because it conflicts with the act of Congress already referred to. Now, at the outset, it is necessary to understand the full import of this conclusion. As it is conceded that the contract does not unreasonably restrain trade, and that if it does not so unreasonably restrain, it is valid under the general law, the decision substantially, is that the act of Congress is a departure from the general principles of law, and by its terms destroys the right of individuals or corporations to enter into very many reasonable contracts. But this proposition, I submit, is tantamount to an assertion that the act of Congress is itself unreasonable. The difficulty of meeting, by reasoning, a premise of this nature is frankly conceded, for, of course, where the fundamental proposition upon which the whole contention rests is that the act of Congress is unreasonable, it would seem conducive to no useful purpose to invoke reason as applicable to and as controlling the construction of a statute which is admitted to be beyond the pale of reason."

The issue thus made as to the proper construction of this statute between the majority and minority of

[19] 166 U. S. 344.

the court is clear. The following quotation, from the majority opinion,[20] is also illuminating:

"Contracts in restraint of trade have been known and spoken of for hundreds of years both in England and in this country, and the term includes all kinds of those contracts which in fact restrain or may restrain trade. Some of such contracts have been held void and unenforceable in the courts by reason of their restraint being unreasonable, while others have been held valid because they were not of that nature. A contract may be in restraint of trade and still be valid at common law. Although valid, it is nevertheless a contract in restraint of trade and would be so described either at common law or elsewhere. By the simple use of the term 'contract in restraint of trade,' all contracts of that nature, whether valid or otherwise, would be included, and not alone that kind of contract which was invalid and unenforceable as being in unreasonable restraint of trade. When, therefore, the body of an act pronounces as illegal *every* contract or combination in restraint of trade or commerce among the several states, etc., the plain and ordinary meaning of such language is not limited to that kind of contract alone which is in unreasonable restraint of trade, but all contracts are included in such language and no exception or limitation can be added without placing in the act that which has been omitted by Congress."

A year or so after the Freight Association, or Trans-Missouri, case above noted, another case arose,

[20] 166 U. S. 328.

usually called the Joint Traffic case, involving substantially the same sort of a contract between railroads as that involved in the Freight Association case, and was decided by the Supreme Court in the same way.[21] Justices White, Gray and Shiras again dissented, and Mr. Justice Field, who had previously dissented, having resigned, his place was taken by Mr. Justice McKenna, who took no part in the decision of the Joint Traffic case.

These two cases, decided in March, 1897, and October, 1898, respectively, *left no doubt* as to the interpretation of the Anti-Trust statute. It made unlawful *any and every* contract in restraint of trade, whether such contract prior to the passage of the Anti Trust statute would have been held void as in unreasonable restraint of trade, or whether it would have been held valid as not unreasonable in its restraint of trade. In the Joint Traffic case, decided in 1898, the Court was asked to reconsider its decision in the Trans-Missouri case, decided in 1897. Upon this point the opinion of the majority of the Court in the Joint Traffic case, says: (p. 573)

"Finally we are asked to reconsider the question decided in the Trans-Missouri case, and to retrace the steps taken therein, ——— The Court is asked to reconsider a question but just decided after a careful in-

[21] United States v. Joint Traffic Association, 171 U. S. 505, 578.

vestigation of the matter involved. There have heretofore been in effect two arguments of precisely the same questions now before the Court, and the same arguments were addressed to us on both those occasions. The report of the Trans-Missouri case shows a dissenting opinion delivered in that case, and that the opinion was concurred in by three other members of the Court. — It was after a full discussion of the questions involved and with the knowledge of the views entertained by the minority as expressed in the dissenting opinion, that the majority of the Court came to the conclusion it did. Soon after the decision, a petition for a rehearing of the case was made supported by a printed argument in its favor and pressed with an earnestness and vigor and at a length which were certainly commensurate with the importance of the case."

The court further said that it had again listened to the same arguments in the case under consideration and again reached the same conclusion. Those interested in having the word "unreasonable" or "undue" read into the Anti-Trust statute after these decisions, turned their attention to Congress and applied as unsuccessfully to Congress as they had to the courts to procure the above suggested modification of the statute. Finally, after various other applications had failed, on April first, 1908, Senator Warner introduced Senate Bill No. 6440 designed among other things to effect the above mentioned purpose. The bill was first referred to the Committe on Interstate Commerce; later it was transferred to the Judiciary Committee of the Senate. On January 26, 1909, the Judiciary Committee reported the bill adversely.[22] In that report it is said:

"The anti-trust act makes it a criminal offense to violate the law, and provides a punishment both by fine and imprisonment. To inject into the act the question of whether an agreement or combination is *reasonable* or *unreasonable* would render the act as a criminal or penal statute indefinite and uncertain, and hence, to that extent, utterly nugatory and void, and would practically amount to a repeal of that part of the act. . . . And while the same technical objection does not apply to civil prosecutions, the injection of the rule of reasonableness or unreasonableness would lead to the greatest variableness and uncertainty in the enforcement of the law. The defense of reasonable restraint would be made in every case, and there would be as many different rules of reasonableness as cases, courts and juries. What one court or jury might deem unreasonable another court or jury might deem reasonable. . . . To amend the anti-trust act, as suggested by this bill, would be to entirely emasculate it, and for all practical purposes render it nugatory as a remedial statute. Criminal prosecutions would not lie and civil remedies would labor under the greatest doubt and uncertainty. The act as it exists is clear, comprehensive, certain and highly remedial. It practically covers the field of Federal jurisdiction, and is in every respect a model law.

22 Senate Report 848, p. 10.

To destroy or undermine it at the present juncture, when combinations are on the increase, and appear to be as oblivious as ever of the rights of the public, would be a calamity."

President Taft, in a special message to Congress said: [23]

"Many people conducting great businesses have cherished a hope and belief that in some way or other a line may be drawn between 'good trusts' and 'bad trusts,' and that it is possible by amendment to the anti-trust law to make a distinction under which good combinations may be permitted to organize, suppress competition, control prices, and do it all legally if only they do not abuse the power by taking too great profit out of the business. They point with force to certain notorious trusts as having grown into power through criminal methods by the use of illegal rebates and plain cheating, and by various acts utterly violative of business honesty and morality, and urge the establishment of some legal line of separation by which 'criminal trusts' of this kind can be punished, and they, on the other hand, be permitted under the law to carry on their business. Now the public, and especially the business public, ought to rid themselves of the idea that such a distinction is practicable or can be introduced into the statute. Certainly under the present anti-trust law no such distinction exists. It has been proposed, however, that the word 'reasonable' should be made a part of the statute, and then that it should be left to the court to

[23] January 7, 1910.

say what is a reasonable restraint of trade, what is a reasonable suppression of competition, what is a reasonable monopoly. I venture to think that this is to put into the hands of the court a power impossible to exercise on any consistent principle which will insure the uniformity of decision essential to good judgment. It is to thrust upon the courts a burden that they have no precedents to enable them to carry, and to give them a power approaching the arbitrary, the abuse of which might involve our whole judicial system in disaster."

It was in this well settled state of the law that the Standard Oil and Tobacco Trust cases were presented to the Supreme Court of the United States in May, 1911.

It is not amiss, before examining the decisions of the Supreme Court itself in these cases to glance at the decisions of the learned lower Courts wherein these cases were considered.

The American Tobacco Company case came up from the United States Circuit Court of Appeals for the Southern District of New York. The Joint Traffic Association case above referred to also originated in that court and had been decided in favor of a construction of the statute substantially the same as that contended for by the minority members of the Supreme Court when the case finally reached that tribunal on appeal.[24]

24 United States v. Joint Traffic Association, 76 Fed. 895; affirmed without opinion, 89 Fed. 1020.

When the American Tobacco Company case, therefore, came before the same Court, in November, 1908, the members of the Court were mindful of their reversal in the Joint Traffic case. Their opinions leave no doubt that *they thoroughly understood* the rule of law which the Supreme Court had announced in that case. Mr. Justice Lacombe said:[25]

"Act July 2, 1890, c. 647, 26 Stat. 209 (U. S. Comp. St. 1901, p. 3200), in its first section, declares to be illegal 'every contract, combination in the form of trust or otherwise, or conspiracy, in restraint of trade or commerce among the several states, or with foreign nations.' That declaration, ambiguous when enacted, is, as the writer conceives, no longer open to construction in the inferior federal courts. Disregarding various dicta and following the several propositions which have been approved by the successive majorities of the Supreme Court, this language is to be construed as prohibiting any contract or combination whose direct effect is to prevent the free play of competition, and thus tend to deprive the country of the services of any number of independent dealers however small. As thus construed the statute is revolutionary. . . . The act may be termed revolutionary, because, before its passage, the courts had recognized a 'restraint of trade' which was held not to be unfair, but permissible, although it operated in some measure to restrict competition. . . . The act as above construed prohibits

[25] 164 Fed. 701.

every contract or combination in restraint of competition."

Mr. Justice Coxe said:[26]

"The anti-trust act embraces and declares to be illegal every contract combination or conspiracy, in whatever form, of whatever nature and whoever may be the parties to it, which directly or necessarily operates in restraint of interstate or international trade or commerce. The act is not limited to *unreasonable* restraints but embraces all direct restraints."

Mr. Justice Noyes said:[27]

"In so far as combinations result from the operation of economic principles, it may be doubtful whether they should be stayed at all by legislation. It may be that the evils in the existing situation should be left to the remedies afforded by the laws of trade. On the other hand, it may be that the protection of the public from the operations of combinations of capital — especially those possessing the element of oppression — requires some measure of governmental intervention. It may be that the present anti-trust statute should be amended and made applicable only to those combinations which *unreasonably* restrain trade — that it should draw a line between those combinations which work for good and those which work for evil. But these are all legislative, and not judicial, questions. It cannot be too clearly borne in mind that this court has nothing to do

26 164 Fed. 707. 27 *Id.*, p. 711.

with the wisdom, justice, or expediency of the statute. Equally true is it that this court, in applying the statute, must follow the decisions of the Supreme Court."

When the Standard Oil case was before the United States Circuit Court of Appeals, in 1909, the question of the construction of the Anti-Trust act was considered in the light of the previous decisions of the United States Supreme Court above noticed, and it is said: [28]

"Repeated discussion and consideration of the purpose and meaning of this act have established, by controlling authority, beyond debate in this tribunal, these pertinent rules for its interpretation and application, to the facts of this case. The test of the legality of a contract or combination under this act is its direct and necessary effect upon competition in interstate or international commerce. If the necessary effect of a contract, combination, or conspiracy is to stifle, or directly and substantially to restrict, free competition in commerce among the States, or with foreign nations, it is a contract, combination, or conspiracy in restraint of that trade, and it violates this law. The parties to it are presumed to intend the inevitable result of their acts, and neither their actual intent nor the *reasonableness* of the restraint imposed may withdraw it from the denunciation of the statute."

From the foregoing review of the authorities, it conclusively appears that when the appeals of the

[28] 173 Fed. 179.

Standard Oil Company and the American Tobacco Company were decided in the Supreme Court, in May, 1911, that Court had three times decided against the construction of the Anti-Trust Statute contended for by those companies, the inferior federal courts had followed and adopted the ruling of the Supreme Court, the Congress of the United States and the President of the United States had said that the construction of the statute declared by the Supreme Court in its majority opinions above noted was sound and wholesome and that the construction contended for by the companies would have made the statute "nugatory" and might, so said the President, "involve our whole judicial system in disaster."

It is not surprising, therefore, that the country was shocked when the long-delayed opinions were handed down, and it was found that the court had adopted the construction of the statute so often rejected and condemned by every department of the government.

The unlawful combinations, at which the statute was aimed were quick to perceive the significance of these decisions. They have also been quick to take advantage of them. The mass of people are slower to realize the full significance of these decisions, but that realization is certain to be eventually brought home to them. The Trans-Missouri case above noted and others must have been decided in favor of the combinations had the rule subsequently announced in the Standard Oil and Tobacco Company cases been applied; and similar combinations must in the future be upheld.

My purpose in gathering together the authorities showing the construction of the anti-trust statute by every department of the government, is not to show that the Supreme Court has reversed itself, nor to convict it of an inconsistency. Had the Court read into the Anti-Trust Act the word "unreasonable" or "undue" when that statute first came before it for consideration, it would not have been less judicial legislation then than it was to do the same thing in the Standard Oil and Tobacco cases. But had those words, or either of them, been read into the statute by the courts in the first instance, the *right of the Court so to do,* which is the question we are here discussing, would not so clearly have been made an issue before the whole country. The fact that this statute had been construed in one way by every department of the government for many years, and that such construction had been repeatedly declared to be the only safe and proper one, had naturally and properly, too, led the people of the country to take the same view of it, and now to change all this, to recant everything that has been said on the subject, and adopt a view many times rejected and declared dangerous, the attention of the whole country is focused upon the Court's action.

Precisely what the Court decided in the Standard Oil case, in the opinion handed down on May 15,

1911, is stated briefly, in that opinion, written by Chief Justice White, as follows: [29]

"The statute under this view evidenced the intent not to restrain the right to make and enforce contracts, whether resulting from combinations or otherwise, which did not *unduly* restrain interstate or foreign commerce, but to protect the commerce from being restrained by methods, whether old or new, which would constitute an interference that is an *undue* restraint."

This is exactly the view taken of the statute, by the same learned Justice in the Trans-Missouri and Joint Traffic cases heretofore discussed, and he adds nothing in the Standard Oil case to the very able argument in support of those views which he submitted in his dissenting opinion in the Trans-Missouri case. The same construction is placed upon the statute in the American Tobacco Company case, but there is this difference noticeable between the opinions in the two cases: In the Standard Oil case, Chief Justice White, in his opinion, seems to admit that the views there expressed conflict with the opinion of the majority of the Court in the Trans-Missouri and Joint Traffic cases, while in the American Tobacco Co. case it is contended that there is no conflict between the rule laid down in that and the Standard Oil case, and the rule announced in the Trans-Missouri and Joint Traffic cases noticed above.

[29] 221 U. S. 1, p. 60.

In the opinion by Mr. Justice White in the Standard Oil case, after trying to harmonize that decision with the two previous cases mentioned, and evidently with unsatisfactory results, it is said: [30]

"And in order, not in the slightest degree to be wanting in frankness, we say that in so far, however, as by separating the general language used in the opinions in the freight association and joint traffic cases from the context and the subject and parties with which the cases were concerned, it may be conceived that the language referred to conflicts with the construction which we give the statute, they are now necessarily limited and qualified."

In the American Tobacco case, however, the learned Chief Justice, writing the opinion for the Court, after construing the statute the same as he had done in the Standard Oil case, said: [31]

"We say the doctrine thus stated was in accord with all the previous decisions of this court, despite the fact that the contrary view was sometimes erroneously attributed to some of the expressions used in two prior decisions. (Trans-Missouri Freight Association and Joint Traffic cases, 166 U. S. 290, and 171 U. S. 505). That such view was a mistaken one was fully pointed out in the Standard Oil case, and is additionally shown by a passage in the opinion in the Joint Traffic case, as follows (171 U. S. 568): 'The act of Congress must

[30] *Id.*, p. 67.

[31] 221 U. S. 106, p. 179.

have a reasonable construction or else there would scarcely be an agreement or contract among business men that could not be said to have indirectly or remotely, some bearing on interstate commerce and possibly to restrain it.' "

Concerning the above quoted statement, Justice Harlan, in his dissenting opinion, in the American Tobacco case, said:[32]

"If I do not misapprehend the opinion just delivered, the court insists that what was said in the opinion in the Standard Oil case was in accordance with our previous decisions in the Trans-Missouri and Joint Traffic cases (166 U. S. 290; 171 U. S. 505), if we resort to reason. This statement surprises me quite as much as would a statement that black was white or white was black."

A pertinent inquiry which arises at this point is: If the doctrine of the Trans-Missouri Freight case, and Joint Traffic case, is the same as that of the Standard Oil and Tobacco cases, why was it necessary for Mr. Justice White, later Chief Justice, to write a long and elaborate dissenting opinion in the first of these cases, and likewise dissent in the second one?

It would certainly seem that the learned Chief Justice was hard pressed for an argument when he quoted from the Joint Traffic case, the language that "*The Act of Congress must have a reasonable con-*

[32] *Id.*, p. 191.

struction," as equivalent to the construction which the majority placed upon the statute in the Standard Oil case and the American Tobacco Co. case. Is the declaration that an Act of Congress must not be construed *unreasonably* equivalent to reading the word *unreasonable* into the statute? To illustrate: — Every State has a law which in substance provides that any person confined in a jail or prison by reason of conviction of some offense, who breaks therefrom, is guilty of a crime. Suppose, however, the jail takes fire and the convict, in order to avoid being burned to death, breaks out of jail. Would any one contend that a court would so construe the statute as to make it apply to such a case and hold that the person so breaking out of jail had committed a crime? Obviously the statute was not intended to cover such a case. The court would give the statute a *reasonable* construction and hold that it was never intended to apply to a case such as I have described. But, would this act of the court be equivalent to reading into the statute the word *unreasonable* so as to make it provide that only a convict who *unreasonably* breaks out of jail shall be guilty of a crime?

Or take another case: — All States have statutes against assault and battery. Suppose a person is drowning or about to fall or throw himself in front of an approaching train and an onlooker by the exercise of violence, and in the case of a person drowning, possibly very great violence, succeeded in rescuing the one in peril. The rescuer clearly committed acts which ordinarily would amount to assault and battery, but would any court, under the circumstances, hold that an assault and battery had been committed? Clearly not. The court would give the statute a *reasonable* construction and say that it was not intended to cover such a case. Must we then treat this action of the court as equivalent to reading into the statute the word *unreasonable* and make it say in effect that only a person, who *unreasonably* commits an assault and battery is guilty of a crime?

The argument of the majority opinion is that, at common law, or in the condition of the law as it existed in this country prior to the passage of the Anti-Trust act, there were two kinds of contracts in restraint of trade, one of which was valid and the other not. One was what the law described as an unreasonable restraint of trade, and the other a reasonable restraint of trade. In this condition, Congress stepped in and said *every* contract in restraint of trade is invalid. Now the majority opinion simply holds that Congress did not mean what it said, but that it only meant every contract which was in *unreasonable* restraint of trade, was invalid. In other words, every contract which was already void under the law, was declared invalid by the statute.

To illustrate: — At common law, there were two

kinds of beatings which a husband could administer to his wife. One was a reasonable beating, which was lawful, the old rule being that the husband could use "a stick as large as his finger but not larger than his thumb." [33] The other was an unreasonable beating, where too large a stick was used or too much violence employed. Now, when a statute steps in and says that any beating of the wife by the husband is unlawful, the Supreme Court, by a parity of reasoning, should hold, if the case of a wifebeater could be brought before it, that the statute did not really mean to prohibit all beating of wives by husbands, but only such beatings as had been held unlawful at common law.

Concerning the contentions of the majority of the Court, as set forth in the opinions of Mr. Justice White, respecting the "rule of reason," Mr. Justice Harlan, in the Tobacco case, said: [34]

"It is scarcely just to the majority in those two cases for the court at this late day to say or to intimate that they interpreted the act of Congress without regard to the 'rule of reason,' or to assume, as the court now does, that the act was, for the first time in the Standard Oil case, interpreted in the 'light of reason.' One thing is certain, 'rule of reason,' to which the court refers, does not justify the perversion of the plain words of an act in order to defeat the will of Congress."

33 Battershall on Domestic Relations, p. 310.
34 *Id.*, p. 191.

This is strong language, especially so when coming from Mr. Justice Harlan and used in an opinion, carefully prepared, and deliberately filed to be a record of the Court's proceeding in that case for all future time.

Further, in the same dissenting opinion, Mr. Justice Harlan says: [35]

"By every conceivable form of expression the majority, in the Trans-Missouri and Joint Traffic cases, adjudged that the act of Congress did not allow restraint of interstate trade to any extent or in any form, and three times it expressly rejected the theory, which had been persistently advanced, that the act should be construed as if it had in it the word 'unreasonable' or 'undue.' But now the court, in accordance with what it denominates the 'rule of reason,' in effect inserts in the act the word 'undue,' which means the same as 'unreasonable,' and thereby makes Congress say what it did not say, what, as I think, it plainly did not intend to say, and what, since the passage of the act, it has explicitly refused to say. It has steadily refused to amend the act so as to tolerate a restraint of interstate commerce even where such restraint could be said to be 'reasonable' or 'due.' In short, the court now, by *judicial legislation,* in effect *amends an act of Congress* relating to a subject over which that department of the government has exclusive cognizance. I beg to say that, in my judgment, the majority, in the former cases, were guided by the 'rule of reason'; for, it may be assumed,

[35] *Id.*, p. 192.

they knew quite as well as others what the rules of reason require when a court seeks to ascertain the will of Congress as expressed in a statute. It is obvious, from the opinions in the former cases, that the majority did not grope about in darkness, but in discharging the solemn duty put on them they stood out in the full glare of the 'light of reason' and felt and said time and again that the court could not, consistently with the Constitution, and would not, usurp the functions of Congress by *indulging in judicial legislation.* They said in express words, in the former cases, in response to the earnest contentions of counsel, that to insert by construction the word 'unreasonable' or 'undue' in the act of Congress would be *judicial legislation.* Let me say, also, that as we all agree that the combination in question was illegal under *any* construction of the anti-trust act, there was not the slightest necessity to enter upon an extended argument to show that the act of Congress was to be read as if it contained the word 'unreasonable' or 'undue.' All that is said in the court's opinion in support of that view is, I say with respect, *obiter dicta,* pure and simple."

The last point made by Mr. Justice Harlan in the above quotation is peculiarly significant. All members of the Court in both the Standard Oil and American Tobacco Co. cases agreed that the contracts and acts there considered were unlawful under any and every view of the statute.

Why then was it necessary to go outside the records in the cases, and outside of anything before the

Court, and anything which the Court could really decide in the cases before it, to indulge in an academic discussion of this statute?

There seems to be but one answer to the question. A majority of the Court, as constituted when the Standard Oil and American Tobacco cases were decided, were ready to agree with the construction of this statute, always contended for by the chief Justice. The men, who standing with Mr. Justice Harlan, previously had constituted a majority of the Court were gone. Chief Justice Fuller, Justice Brown, Justice Brewer and Justice Peckham, who, with Justice Harlan, constituted a majority of the Court when the Trans-Missouri and Joint Traffic cases were decided, were no longer members of the Court. Their places had been taken by new men. Four lawyers, recently elevated to the Bench, agreed with the view of this statute, always contended for by Mr. Justice White, and three times rejected by the Court, and the policy of the government, as to combinations and monopolies in restraint of trade, was changed in a day. This was done also without any question being presented to the Court, that required or called for the opinion rendered. On the 14th day of May, 1911, *every* contract, in whatever form, in restraint of trade among the States or with foreign nations, was illegal and every combination built upon such contract or contracts was illegal, and subject to be destroyed by the judgment of a Court, and the participants therein punished as criminals. On the fifteenth day of May, 1911, all this was changed, and it was *only such contracts* as some court might hold to be in "undue" or "unreasonable" restraint of trade that were unlawful. It was only combinations built upon such "unreasonable" contracts that were unlawful, and only participants in such last named combinations that became criminals. Scores of most important contracts and transactions that violated the law on the 14th day of May, 1911, were valid on the succeeding day. What it was not lawful to do on the 14th day of May, 1911, to restrain commerce and destroy competition, it was lawful to do on the succeeding day.

What had occurred?

No new law had been passed by Congress. No new statute or new or novel state of facts even had been presented to a Court for consideration. The Supreme Court, in deciding that certain acts violated the statute, had simply stepped aside from the decision in hand, and said in substance that certain other acts equally condemned by the language of the statute, and the previous decisions of the Court, would not in the future be held to violate the statute. That was all. Had the members of the Court met and done this without deciding any case at all, I suppose no one would have defended their act. But as a practical matter, wherein lies the difference? The important fact is that the Court, as Mr. Justice

Harlan shows, amended the statute and did so by reading into it language that was not written there by Congress. If the Court, under the Constitution, has no authority to do this, what does it matter whether at the time its members were engaged in deciding a case or not?

One of the most important results of this decision will be that it will bring home to the public mind the conviction that the courts must be reckoned with as a law-making branch of the government. Whether the people will follow the illustrious example of President Taft, who after the court's decision upheld the construction of the statute he formerly vigorously condemned,[36] remains to be seen.

The evidence to date indicates that they will not

[36] As we have already seen, President Taft, in a special message to Congress, under date of Jan. 7, 1910, condemned in the most vigorous language, the proposition that Congress should amend the statute by inserting in it the words the court has now read into it and of such action, declared that it would give the courts "A power approaching the arbitrary, the abuse of which might involve our whole judicial system in disaster." On June 21, 1911, following the decisions in the Standard Oil and Tobacco Company cases, in a speech at the Yale Alumni Luncheon, President Taft said: "It has fallen to my lot to have five members of that court (the Supreme Court), bear my commission. . . . I believe these decisions (Standard Oil and American Tobacco Co. decisions) have done, and will continue to do great good to all the business of the country and that they have laid down a line of distinction which it is not difficult for honest and intelligent business men to follow."

do so. Even those who rejoice at a construction of the anti-trust law which practically destroys it, generally conceded that the Court was obliged to legislate in order to reach the desired end. Mr. Justice Grosscup of the United States Circuit Court of Appeals, in writing of the decisions said:[37]

"It would be mere hypocrisy to say that the court has not turned upon itself. What the court fourteen years ago said was not in the act the court now says *is* in the act. Meantime, not a letter of the act has been changed. What has changed is the attitude of the public mind — the public mind, informed by this fourteen years of experience. There are windows in the Supreme Court room from which what is going on in the world outside is in plain sight."

Again the same eminent jurist says:[38]

"From the view-point of a larger number of those to whom this inquiry is a matter of deep concern, perhaps a large majority yet, the Sherman Act, as it now stands interpreted, will look like a gun from which the load has been extracted. As a *weapon* it will look dismantled. As a mere weapon it *is* dismantled. If in the interests of the ordinary man these modern economic methods and tendencies must be overhauled and destroyed — if union of effort and capital solely because it is effort and capital *in union* must be circumvented —

[37] *North American Review*, July, 1911, Vol. CXCIV, No. 1, p. 3.

[38] *Id.*, p. 9.

this latest decision has drawn the load of the only gun thus far trained against the enemy."

Mr. James M. Beck, for many years the United States Attorney for the Eastern District of Pennsylvania, and Assistant Attorney-General of the United States, after pointing out the hardships involved in enforcing the Anti-Trust Act as it was written, has this to say:[39]

"Such was the real crisis which confronted the Supreme Court when it considered the Standard Oil and Tobacco cases. It could do little to save a dangerous situation unless it was prepared to disregard its own precedents and conform the interpretation of the statute to the reasonable necessities of the American people and the obvious tendencies of an age preëminently of combination. It chose a course, difficult to justify, as Justice Harlan's powerful dissenting opinion well shows, on strictly technical grounds, and with due regard to the principle of *stare decisis,* but amply justified upon the broader consideration of the public welfare."

Again he says:[40]

"Chief Justice White, in my judgment the ablest dialectician of the Supreme Court since Marshall's time, justifies the assumption of legislative power to determine what is reasonable in the matter of economics by referring to the fact that the courts have heretofore de-

[39] *Id.*, p. 60. [40] *Id.*, p. 64.

termined whether a litigant has been found guilty of fraud."

Of this reasoning Mr. Beck says:

"I confess that I cannot follow the analogy."

Mr. Samuel Untermyer, a well known organizer of and counsel for many corporations, says:[41]

"That the Court has retraced its steps and has unsaid and undone much of what was decided in the Trans-Missouri and Joint Traffic Association cases is, however, hardly open to discussion. . . . With all due respect to that august tribunal which the members of the Bar so justly revere, the progressive, constructive policy which we so profoundly admire, one is at times disposed to regret that the traditions of the Court do not seem to permit that it admit its fallibility and frankly announce that it has decided to reject, overrule, or change the law laid down in its earlier decisions, when that is in fact its real purpose, instead of resorting to circumlocution and to distinctions that do not always distinguish. . . . We may, if we please, criticise and denounce that exercise of power as judicial legislation and as being in theory lawless and dangerous and contrary to the spirit of our institutions, as Mr. Justice Harlan and other eminent jurists of that great Court have from time to time arraigned it."

But Mr. Untermyer concludes that the end justifies the means and says he desires to add his "tribute

[41] *Id.*, pp. 78–9.

to the Court for its broad and statesmanlike construction of the Sherman Law."

It is safe to say that when gentlemen like the foregoing frankly concede that the Court is exercising legislative power, the mass of people will soon recognize the same fact. Then it will follow, that since judges legislate, they will be treated as legislators. They will be criticized frankly and freely. They will learn what the public sentiment demands, not through their "windows" but through their doors. They will be elected and not appointed. Their terms of office will be brief. Their views on questions likely to come before them will be known and proclaimed in advance. All this must follow the conviction in the public mind that judges have, in effect, become legislators. If this is revolutionary, the judges are the revolutionists.

CHAPTER V

WHY THE PEOPLE DISTRUST THE COURTS

(D) The poor man is not on an equality with the rich one before the courts.

THE above statement, which is uniformly accepted as true, is the most serious of the charges against the courts. The manner in which the courts come by the powers they exercise would excite less comment if the power itself had been used only for the public good. It would be easier to forget that the Constitution gives the courts no power to invalidate acts of Congress if such power had been exercised solely to protect the people from harsh and unpopular measures. If it were generally believed that laws were improved by judicial amendment, the exercise by the courts of the power to amend statutes might be regarded as less dangerous, but the belief that the acts of the Judiciary in amending statutes are almost always exercised in behalf of special interests and intended to defeat the popular will, adds bitterness to the public's condemnation of judicial legislation.

Wealth has certain legitimate advantages in litigation which cannot be overcome. So long as the rich litigant can employ better counsel, prepare his case better, and endure more easily the "law's delays" he will always have great advantage over his poorer opponent. This subject, however, we are not discussing, and it is poor service to the cause of judicial reform to point out these conditions as constituting real grounds of complaint against the courts. But it would seem that judges, mindful of this inherent inequality, would have sought by their rulings not to increase, even if they did not lessen, the already great advantage of the more powerful party. This appears not to have been the case. The complaint against the courts at this point is much more fundamental than any matter of procedure, or expense, or delay.

The charge against the courts is that their judges habitually think in the terms of the rich and powerful.

The training, sympathies, experiences and general view of life of most judges has made this inevitable.

The process of thinking, always on the side of vested interests, of the established order, and of the powerful individuals and corporations continued through a century has built up a system of law barbarous in its injustice and inequality.

It would be hard to imagine a case decided a hundred years ago involving the relative rights and duties of capital and labor, or of employer and employé, which ought to be a precedent or controlling authority upon the same questions to-day.

Yet the fact is, that the courts have not only held tenaciously to the old dogmas, but have extended the hard rules of law then applicable to the controversies mentioned, so as to make them bear more heavily upon the poorer and weaker classes.

Not only this, but when Congress and Legislatures have intervened to abolish the hardships of the old rules of law by humane statutes, the courts, as we have seen, have constantly thwarted the legislative intent, by invalidating many of such laws and by misinterpreting others.

The decision of long ago has become the precedent for to-day. The mere suggestion of a judge in one case, not necessary to its decision, is seized upon and set forth as the law of the next. Principles applied to the facts of one case are carried over and made to decide another case with very different facts. And always the process has gone on discriminating in favor of the strong and wealthy, and against the poor and weak. This process has continued, until the complaint to-day is directed, not against the "bad law" of the erroneous decision, but against the "good law" of the correct decision. It is not the occasional decision, contrary to precedent, that works the injustice, but the uniform current of decisions in line with the precedents.

President Lincoln said:[1]

"Labor is prior to and independent of capital. Capital is only the fruit of labor and could never have existed if labor had not existed first. Labor is the superior of capital and deserves much higher consideration."

The above sentiment of President Lincoln, undoubtedly expresses the conviction of the American public, to-day, even better than when it was uttered. Yet the converse of that sentiment fairly states the attitude of the courts; and it is the decisions necessary to fortify and defend that attitude which have, in a large measure, bred a popular distrust of the courts, the more serious because largely suppressed.

Since what I am saying is a matter of record, and not of opinion, I will let the cases speak for themselves, using those which illustrate the condition of the law as applied to employer and employé, or (to use the language of the books) master and servant; disputes between labor and capital and, what for want of a better term, is usually described as vested interests.

In 1837, there lived in one of the rural communities of England, a butcher named Fowler. He seems to have followed his worthy occupation with some success, for at the time mentioned, his business had prospered to the point where he employed two

[1] Message to Congress, Dec., 1861.

servants in it, and owned a cart and horse used to peddle meat to his various patrons. The name of one of the servants which has been immortalized in the law books was Priestley. At the time mentioned, Priestley and his fellow servant, were engaged in driving the cart of Mr. Fowler, loaded with meat, along the road in their work of supplying the customers. The cart suddenly, and without any warning, broke down, and, we are informed, one of the legs of Mr. Priestley, who was at the time riding on the cart, was thereby severely injured. Mr. Priestley sued Mr. Fowler in the Courts of England to recover damages for the injury to his leg. He was the first employé or servant who ever had the hardihood to bring an action under the English law to recover damages from his master, on any similar state of facts.[2] Mr. Priestley in his complaint stated. (I quote from the case) —

"That the plaintiff was the servant of the defendant in his trade as a butcher. . . . That the defendant did not use proper care to see that the van (butcher's cart) was in a proper state of repairs, and was not overloaded; and that in consequence of the defendant's neglect in each of his duties, the van gave way and broke down and the plaintiff was thrown to the ground,"

and his leg injured, etc. The jury gave a verdict for the plaintiff for one hundred pounds. The Judge,

[2] Priestley v. Fowler, 3 Mee. & Well., p. 1.

however, arrested the judgment, or, as we would say, set the verdict aside. This action of the judge was held proper on the appeal. Lord Abinger, who wrote the opinion on the appeal, said:

"It is admitted that there is no precedent for the present action by a servant against a master. We are, therefore, to decide the question upon the general principles, and in doing so we are at liberty to look at the consequences of a decision the one way or the other. If the master be liable to the servant in this action, the principle of that liability will be found to carry us to an alarming extent. . . . If the owner of the carriage is therefore responsible for the sufficiency of his carriage to his servant, he is responsible for the negligence of his coach maker, or for a defect in the harness arising from the negligence of the harness maker, or for drunkenness, negligence, or want of skill in the coachman. . . . The master, for example, would be liable to the servant for the negligence of a chambermaid for putting him into a damp bed. . . . The inconvenience, not to say the absurdity, of these consequences affords a sufficient argument against the application of this principle to the present case. . . . He (the master) is no doubt bound to provide for the safety of his servant in the course of his employment to the best of his judgment, information and belief. The servant is not bound to risk his safety in the service of the master, and may, if he thinks fit, decline any service in which he reasonably apprehends injury to himself; and in most of the cases in which danger may be incurred, if not all, he is just as likely to be acquainted with the probability and extent of it as the master. . . . In fact, to allow this sort of an action to prevail would be an encouragement to omit that diligence and caution which he is in duty bound to exercise on the behalf of his master to protect him against the misconduct or negligence of others who serve him."

With this decision, there was born into the world of the English Law the twin propositions, *first:* that a servant or employé must be held, when he enters the employ of another, to have assumed the risks of such employment, and *second:* that the master is not liable for damage to one servant or employé, caused by the negligence of a fellow servant or employé. These principles of law, thus originating, were carried to this country the following year [3] and soon became the law of the land.

These principles of law, devised by an English Judge nearly a hundred years ago, in order to protect a master from liability for injury to his servant caused by the breaking of the horse cart on which he was riding, as applied by our courts, have saved countless millions of dollars to the employing classes in this country, while they have killed and made paupers of untold thousands of laborers and their wives and

[3] Farwell v. Boston and Worcester R. R. Corporation, 4 Metc. (Mass.), 49; Brown v. Maxwell, 6 Hill (New York), 592–4.

children. These principles, as applied by our courts have bred in some of the employing classes, a reckless and wanton disregard of the safety and lives of the employed, and have aroused in the latter a class hatred which is a constant menace to our society and government. No one can estimate the suffering, or count the army of the dead and crippled, born of these dogmas of a primitive industrial time. I quote from the recent report of the American Association for Labor Legislation,[4] where, referring to the statistics of railway casualties compiled for the year 1910, it is said:

"We find that nine men were killed each twenty-four hours, and that one was injured or killed every seven minutes. To be specific as to casualties as they occur in the engine, train, and yard service, is to say that one man was killed for each two hundred and five employed, and one was injured for every nine employed."

War is safe compared to railroading in this country. I continue the quotation:

"What do the railways pay? No one knows; but it is reasonable to say that ten per cent. of injuries and deaths for which compensation is paid, is the answer, and the average amount paid is low. . . . The miners claim that four men are killed in America to one in Europe, and it is admitted that mining ordinarily

[4] Publication No. 12, p. 43, proceedings of the Fourth Annual Meeting, January, 1911.

and normally ought to be accompanied with less danger here than abroad. Structural iron and steel workers and electrical workers stand a heavy loss in death and disability only to be guessed at in the total, for we lack full statistics covering these occupations. It has been estimated that annually four thousand Pennsylvania miners are killed or injured, and the records of Allegheny County, in which the great iron and steel industries of the Pittsburg district are located, showed ten thousand casualties a year, a large proportion of which were deaths or total disablements, and eighty per cent. of which were inflicted upon men under forty years of age. Few of these casualties have hope of recovery because no one was at fault, and the others have been divided among a half dozen causes, few of which contained hope of recovery from the courts."

The laborer assumed the risk of the employment. From the same report I quote again: [5]

"A system of almost perfect mechanical production has been installed, and the man must keep pace with it. So much must be produced per man, per machine per hour, and the man knows if he falls below the minimum of production he will lose his job, and a job is a job even in this land of opportunity. He knows the inexorable rule. The result is that to change a gear, shift a belt, adjust a feed, or any one of the thousands of ways that are offered the man to take a chance and keep his machine going without loss of time, are accepted at

[5] P. 45.

the price of safety, and he pays the price. The employer pays nothing. The occupational diseases that must be assumed by the employé, of which there is really no record, must be considered among the casualties, although they have little hope of compensation. All of them add to the burden of general human misery arising from suspended or decreased wages. So we say advisedly, until sane rules of employment regulate industry, until it costs more to kill a man than to protect him, until the man and the machine are brought closer to the relative endurance of each other, and safety devices are installed that automatically will prevent accidents, we shall have an annual casualty roll that will warrant a repetition of the statement, that the mines are stained with the blood of their victims; every skyscraper is cemented with the blood and brawn of its builders; every large enterprise is baptized in the blood of its workmen.

"Does it not appeal to you that there is an underlying cause other than negligence that is responsible for the casualty record? That a man works for another does not mean that he is indifferent to physical and mental pain. The general toll of industry is estimated at anywhere from one-half million upward annually, but we are unable to do more than estimate, for outside of railways no reliable statistics are available. . . . In a general way we realize what it means to the man who is left helpless and hopeless. One can, in a way, imagine the physical suffering which we believe can in part be compensated, but God alone knows the mental depths of despair to which the one time physically perfect man is plunged when disability overtakes and threatens his earning capacity, for in this day he knows when he cannot work he becomes a pauper. I have seen strong men weep like children when they were out of work temporarily, and their families were forced to limited living. What must it mean, then, to the one who in a moment knows he is done forever? . . . It is inhuman to compel the employé to accept the responsibility for accident in exchange for the opportunity to work. That responsibility belongs exclusively to the employer.

"American industry has been protected in every way possible by law and court decision, but the employés, the foundation of American industry, have been thrown aside as scrap, and their bruised and broken bodies added to the long roll of human wreckage to attest to the unrecompensed sacrifices made in its behalf."

Had the doctrine of Priestley v. Fowler been confined to the facts or situation involved, it would have done little harm and would now be merely one of the curiosities of the law. But our courts have taken the doctrine of that case, and made it control and decide cases differing from it in their facts as much as the simple butcher's cart, drawn by a horse to furnish meat to the countryside, differs from the modern ice-packed refrigerator car which traverses a continent in a few hours. Under the rule of assumed risk, the courts say that the section hand injured by collision with a wild engine, of the approach of which he had no warning, cannot recover, for this is one of the risks of the business.[6]

Coupling cars in motion is a risk brakemen must assume.[7] Failure of the railroad to maintain gates or signals at a crossing, although required to do so, is a risk the trainmen must assume, if they might have known of the company's omission.[8] Any unsafe and careless custom of the employer, if open to the observation of an employé, in the opinion of a Court who considers the matter after the accident, is a risk the employé must assume.[9] Railroad employés must assume the risk of being killed by structures or obstructions maintained dangerously near the track if a Court can say they had notice of the danger.[10] Passing frequently on a rapidly moving train, while engaged in his duties, an object dangerously near the track, enables the Court to say that the employé had notice of the danger.[11] Improper ventilation of tunnels is a risk to be assumed by the workmen therein.[12] If the employé has merely what the court calls " means of knowing the dangers in-

[6] Sullivan v. Fitchburg, etc., R. R. Co., 161 Mass. 125.

[7] Ferguson v. Central Ia. Ry., 58 Ia. 293.

[8] Bancroft v. Boston & Me. Ry. (N. H.), 30 Atl. 409.

[9] Hughes v. Winona & St. P. Ry. Co., 27 Minn. 137.

[10] Gaffney v. N. Y., etc., Ry., 15 R. I. 456; Needham v. Louisville, etc., Ry., 85 Ky. 423; Perigo v. C. R., etc., Ry., 52 Ia. 276; Sisco v. L. & H. Ry., 145 N. Y. 296.

[11] Boyd v. Harris (Pa. St.), 35 Atl. 222.

[12] Balt. & P. Ry. Co. v. State, 75 Md. 152.

volved" he is deemed to assume the risk of all such dangers and to have waived any claim against the Master for injuries resulting therefrom.[13]

Even statutes requiring dangerous machinery to be covered or guarded may be disobeyed by the employer, and little children employed about such ungarded machinery are held to have assumed the risk.[14] The same rule applies to women.[15] Even a statute declaring that "the question whether the employé understood and assumed the risk" shall be one of fact,[16] will be disregarded by the courts if only the danger is obvious enough.[17]

Similarly applying the fellow servant rule, the courts declare that the mechanic in the shop, and the engineer on the engine are fellow servants, so that the latter cannot recover for injuries, if they are caused by the negligence of the former.[18] The conductor on a train, and the foreman of a section crew are fellow servants for the purpose of preventing recovery by the latter against the company for injuries caused by the conductor's negligence.[19] The fellow

[13] Crown v. Orr, 140 N. Y. 450; Davidson v. So. Pac. Co., 44 Fed. 476.

[14] Higgins v. O'Keefe, 79 Fed. 900; White v. Wittemann Lith. Co., 131 N. Y. 631.

[15] Knisley v. Pratt, 148 N. Y. 372.

[16] Sec. 3, Chapt. 600, N. Y. laws of 1902.

[17] Milligan v. Clayville Kn. Co., 137 App. Div. 383.

[18] Mobile, etc., Ry. v. Thomas, 42 Ala. 672.

[19] So. Pac. Ry. v. McGill (Ariz.), 44 Pac. 302.

servant rule prevents recovery for the death of miners who are killed by the explosion of fire damp ignited by an employé but negligently and knowingly permitted by the owner of the mines to accumulate.[20] The fireman on his locomotive is a fellow servant of a train despatcher, though they may be thousands of miles apart.[21]

So also a track inspector, whose negligent inspection of the track causes the train to fall through a bridge and kills the engineer is the fellow servant of the latter, and the railway company is not liable.[22] Even the foreman of the laborers, with full power to hire and discharge and superintend the work is a fellow servant with them, when the latter are killed or injured by the foreman's negligence, and the company therefore is not liable.[23]

So the list might be indefinitely extended, showing how the courts have built up a body of law to protect the employing classes from liability for injuries to their employés, which a humane and enlightened public sentiment long ago became convinced the employers should bear. That England, wherein the doctrine of assumed risk and the fellow servant rule

20 Berns v. Coal Co., 27 W. Va. 285.

21 Millsaps v. Louisville, etc., Ry., 69 Miss. 423; N. O. J. & G. N. R. R. Co. v. Hughes, 49 Miss. 258, 289.

22 Warner v. Erie Ry., 39 N. Y. 468.

23 N. Pac. R. R. Co. v. Peterson, 162 U. S. 346. See also, N. Pac. R. R. Co. v. Charless, 162 U. S. 359.

originated, long ago discarded both, seems to have meant nothing to our courts.[24]

The next great service of the courts to the employing class was in nullifying and destroying statutes, state and federal, passed to correct the injustice and barbarities of the old law, as applied to the laboring classes. In the footnote I set out a few of the many cases in addition to these already noted illustrating the extent to which the courts have gone to break down this kind of legislation.[25] Every State in the Union which has passed progressive labor legislation, such as the Factory Acts, looking to the protection of the lives and health of workers, and statutes changing the ancient rules of law relating to master and servant, which our courts have

[24] English Employers' Liability Act of 1880, 43 and 44 Victoria, Chapt. 42.

[25] Nappa v. Erie Ry. Co., 195 N. Y. 176, 184; Guilmartin v. Solvay Process Co., 189 N. Y. 490, 494; Gallagher v. Newman, 190 N. Y. 444, 447–8; Hope v. Scranton & Lehigh Coal Co., 120 A. D. 595; Cashman v. Chase, 156 Mass. 342; Quinlan v. Lackawanna Steel Co., 107 A. D. 176, affirmed 191 N. Y. 329; Finnigan v. N. Y. Contracting Co., 194 N. Y. 244; Baker v. Empire Wire Co., 102 A. D. 125.

In New York it is necessary to constantly amend the labor statutes in order to keep up with the decisions of the courts. See also, articles in *Bench & Bar* for April, 1908, 13 *Bench & Bar*, p. 17; also article on the "Recent Amendment of the Labor Law," *Bench & Bar* for August, 1910, 22 *Bench & Bar*, p. 45. Carl v. Bangor, etc., Ry. Co., 43 Me. 269; Lutz v. Atlantic, etc., Ry. Co., 53 Am. and Eng. Ry. cases, 478; Proctor v. Ry., 64 Mo. 112.

applied to employers and employés, will furnish many other illustrations of judicial hostility to this kind of legislation.

It is at this point that the issue between the people and the courts has become clearly defined.

So long as the judges confined themselves to dealing in general principles, and were always able to cite some previous case which seemed to excuse the decision in the case at hand, the public suspended judgment, and thought possibly the courts were bound by precedents, and that they might be excused for adhering to the ancient and discredited rules of law.

But when after much agitation and extended investigation, plain statutes were passed, correcting the abuses of the old laws, and the people saw those statutes, again and again, either nullified by the courts entirely, or so interpreted as to make them fail of their purpose, the period for suspended judgment ended and the public made up its mind.

The public believes now that the courts are against those progressive measures and policies which the majority of the people favor.

While a number of individual judges, particularly some of those on the Federal Bench, have recently been subjected to severe criticism for their decisions in labor cases, I feel that this is a superficial view. Some judges are, of course, more reactionary than others, but the fact is that with a few great exceptions, the bench, as a whole, has shown itself not only out of sympathy with the new economic and industrial legislation of the country, but positively hostile to it.

In Volume 42 of *Studies in History, Economics and Public Laws,* edited by the Faculty of Political Science of Columbia University and published in 1911, George Gorham Groat, Ph.D., discusses at great length, the "Attitude of American Courts in Labor Cases."

This work is very conservative, and deals principally with the attitude of the courts in those labor cases, where the principles of law have not yet been settled; consequently the author is able to write hopefully of some of the rules of law, which he thinks the courts may finally declare applicable to this class of litigation. At page 360, however, the author says:

"If the differences, the confusion, the conflicting decisions and the general feeling of dissatisfaction are to any extent to be removed, these facts must be realized. First, it is undeniable that a certain theory underlies the legal view which is not generally accepted outside of legal circles. This theory is that law is based on certain principles of justice that are eternal, and immutable. . . . A consequence is, that the common law brought over from the past, into the present, is expressed quite entirely in phrases that have but little, if any, present application."

Continuing, the author says:

"A second great fact is that of industrial change. This is so generally recognized, as to make anything more than the mere statement of it, unnecessary. . . . Bringing these facts together — fixed theory of the law, and changing conditions of society, written constitutions based on early philosophy, and industrial and social structure, based on a later philosophy — the real underlying nature of the difficulty appears. Judges are trained primarily in the law, and are bound by habits of thought to follow the beaten paths marked out by the precedents of earlier years. Laws (statutes) upon which they pass opinions, are on the contrary essentially adapted to present day conditions."

The author then quotes an article in the *Columbia Law Review*, Volume 3, page 344, May, 1905, as expressive of his own views, as follows:

"To-day for the first time, the common law finds itself arrayed against the people; for the first time instead of securing for them what they most prize, they know it chiefly as something that continually stands between them and what they desire. . . . There is a feeling that it (the common law) prevents everything, and does nothing. . . . It exhibits too great a respect for the individual and for the intrenched position in which our legal and political history has put him, and too little respect for the needs of society, when they come in conflict with the individual, to be in touch with the present age."

After a further discussion of the unsatisfactory condition of the law in labor cases, as evidenced by the opinions of the courts, the author says:

> "In such a situation as has been outlined, it is impossible to secure with any promptness, a satisfactory adjustment between the opinions of courts and the needs of a live industrial society."

Akin to the doctrine of "assumed risk" and the "fellow servant rule" just discussed, is the doctrine of "contributory negligence." As a money saving device, to employers, this rule is almost equal in value to the "assumed risk" and "fellow servant" rule and its justice seems more apparent. It sounds fair to say that an employé who, by his negligence, brings an injury upon himself, should not recover from his employer on account of such injury. This is the rule of contributory negligence, and when properly applied, between parties, on approximately equal terms, there is much to be said in its favor. It was intended, of course, that a jury should always determine the question of fact, whether the plaintiff was guilty of contributory negligence or not. The rule, however, as actually applied in practice, has become one of great hardship because the judges have come to determine the question of negligence to a large extent, thus really exercising the function of the jury, and the alternative often presented to an employé of losing his job or doing an act which can be called negligent, deprives the parties of that substantial equality which is necessary to any fair application of the rule.

A recent rule promulgated by a leading Railway Company is as follows:

" . . . employés before they attempt to make couplings or to uncouple, will examine and see that the cars and engines to be coupled or uncoupled, couplers, draw-heads and other appliances connected therewith, ties, rails, tracks and roadbeds, are in good safe condition. . . . They must exercise great care in coupling and uncoupling cars. In all cases, sufficient time must be taken to avoid accident or personal injury." [26]

Now note the letter of instruction the superintendent in charge of the employés of that Railway sends out for the actual direction of the men: [27]

"Entirely too much time is being lost, especially on local trains, due to the train and engine men not taking advantage of conditions in order to gain time doing work, switching and unloading and loading freight. Neither must they wait until the train stops to get men in position. It is also of the utmost importance that engine men be alive, prompt to take signals, and make quick moves. In this respect it is only necessary to call your attention to the old adage, which is a true one, that when train or engine men do not make good

[26] *American Labor Legislation Review*, Vol. I, No. 1, p. 42, issued by the American Association for Labor Legislation.

[27] *Id.*, p. 43.

on local trains, it thoroughly demonstrates those men are detrimental to the service, as well as their own personal interests, and such men, instead of being assigned to other runs, should be dispensed with. I am calling your attention to these matters with a view to invigorating energy and ambition, in order that your families, who are dependent on you to make a success, shall not some day point the finger of scorn at you, and that the public may not be able to say, you lost your position due to the lack of energy and interest in your own personal welfare, for which you can consistently place the responsibility on no one but yourself."

The rule is general, and is for the defense of the company. The letter is private, and is for the guidance of the men, and they soon learn that it is the spirit of the letter and not of the rule which must be obeyed, if they hold their jobs. The rule of contributory negligence takes no account of the fact that most employés to-day do their work in the presence of the danger, on the one hand of being discharged if they take the time to be cautious, and on the other hand of being crippled or killed if they act with the haste necessary to secure the approval of their superiors. The Court, however, determines the question of negligence after the accident in the quiet and comfort and security of the court room, upon "due deliberation," and with all the facts carefully brought out, and the judge can always feel sure, that no matter how hasty or how deliberate he may be in the matter, his job is secure. Then also, the courts in some of the States, for example, New York, require the plaintiff in an action for personal injuries, to prove that the victim of the injury was free from negligence at the time of the accident, for which damages were sought to be recovered.[28] When, therefore, the unfortunate victim of the injury is dead, it often happens that no such proof can be furnished. After much agitation, this rule was changed by statute in New York, in 1910.[29] Concerning this change in the law, the Editor of *Bench & Bar* recently said:[30]

"A fundamental rule in the law of negligence in this State existing from the earliest times is abrogated. The practical importance of the change is manifest. The number of negligence actions which have failed through inability of the plaintiff to give evidence of his, or his decedent's freedom from contributory negligence can only be conjectured; but they must number many hundreds."

How the courts will deal with this statute remains to be seen.

28 Whalen v. Citizens' Gas Light Co., 151 N. Y. 70.

29 Chapt. 352 of the Laws of 1910 amending the Labor Law, Sec. 202a. The above section is as follows:

"On the trial of an action brought by an employé or his personal representative to recover damages for negligence arising out of and in the course of such employment, contributory negligence of the injured employé shall be a defense to be so pleaded and proved by the defendant."

30 *Bench & Bar* for August, 1910, p. 51.

A recent case illustrating the length to which the courts have gone in usurping the function of the jury in dealing with the question of contributory negligence is that of Mastin v. City of New York.[31] The difference between the province of the Court and Jury in this class of cases is recognized by all the authorities and is usually stated as follows:

> "When reasonable and intelligent men may differ as to what facts have been established, or may draw antagonistic inferences from undisputed facts, the case is one for a jury." [32]

In the case of Mr. Mastin, above referred to, it appears that in 1910, he was injured on the streets of New York, by a vehicle under the control, and in the service of the City. The principal defense of the City was that plaintiff was guilty of contributory negligence. The trial judge, however, under proper instructions, submitted the case to the jury, who returned a verdict for the plaintiff. An appeal was taken to the Appellate Division, where the judgment was affirmed, one judge dissenting. The City then appealed to the Court of Appeals, which, by a vote of four to three, held that as a matter of law, the plaintiff was guilty of contributory negligence, and could not recover. It thus appears that the trial judge, four judges in the Appellate Division, and

[31] Vol. 201, N. Y., p. 81.

[32] Smith v. N. Y. C. & H. R. R. R. Co., 177 N. Y. 224, 229.

three judges in the Court of Appeals, eight in all, agreed that the evidence presented a question of fact for the decision of a jury, and one judge in the Appellate Division and four in the Court of Appeals, five in all, held the contrary. Nevertheless, the decision was that no question was presented for a jury to pass upon, thus holding that reasonable and intelligent men could not differ as to what facts had been established or as to the inferences which could be drawn therefrom, and therefore, that the plaintiff, as a matter of law, was guilty of contributory negligence and could not recover. The logic of this decision seems to be that four judges of the Court of Appeals, must have held that the eight judges,— three of the Court of Appeals, four of the Appellate Division, and the trial judge — were not "reasonable and intelligent men," otherwise it would not have been possible to take the case from the jury. This case shows, better than any extended discussion could do, the extent to which judges have gone in order to take question of negligence and contributory negligence from the jury and pass on them themselves.

We turn now to another branch of the law which, in recent years, has been the subject of much controversy and one wherein the decisions of the courts have aroused the hostility of a large proportion of our people. I refer to the decisions relating to Labor Unions, and particularly contests between labor and capital as manifested in strikes, boycotts, lockouts and other aggressive and retaliatory tactics to which each side has resorted.

From the first "Statute of Laborers" [33] passed in 1349, to the present time, the law has always discriminated against those engaged in manual labor, or what we now call the "working classes." This early statute, in the reign of Edward III., the first one upon the subject, grew out of the scarcity of labor resulting from the wars and pestilence of that period. It fixed the wages which any laborer might ask and receive, and punished with severe penalties any laborer who asked for more than the rate fixed by law, and any employer who paid more than the law provided for. This and the statute passed the next year provided:

"That every man and woman of what condition he be, free or bond, able in body and within the age of three score years, (if he have no means of his own) if he in convenient service, his estate considered, be required to serve, he shall be bounden to serve him which so shall him require."

A distinguished writer on the criminal law of England, concerning these statutes, said:

"The main object of these statutes was to check the rise in wages consequent upon the great pestilence called the black death." [34]

[33] 23 Edw. III.

[34] *Stephen's History of the Criminal Law of England,* **Vol. III, p. 204.**

By many subsequent statutes, these provisions were reënacted and others passed, even more stringent, and by which the hours of labor were fixed, in some instances from five A. M. to eight P. M. By these early statutes, laborers who left their work and went into another county were liable to be arrested by the Sheriff and brought back, and all alliances and unions between laborers were prohibited.[35]

In 1548 a more general statute was passed which forbade laborers to *conspire*

> "not to make or do their work, but at a certain price or rate"

under penalty of loss of an ear and of being declared infamous.[36] In 1720 an act was passed declaring all agreements of various laborers

> "for advancing their wages or for lessening their usual hours of work"

to be null and void, and imposing the penalty of imprisonment for entering into such agreements.[37] As late as the year 1800 a statute was passed [38] which provided imprisonment with hard labor for the workman who

> "enters into any combination to obtain an advance of wages or lessen or alter the hours of work, . . . or

[35] See statutes of 1360, 1368, 1388.
[36] 2 and 3 Edw. VI, c. 15.
[37] 7 Geo. I, 1, c. 13.
[38] 40 Geo. III, c. 60.

who hinders any employer from employing any person as he thinks proper or who, being hired, refuses without any just or reasonable cause, to work with any other journeyman or workmen employed or hired to work."

Severe penalties were also inflicted upon persons who attended meetings held for the purpose of collecting money to advance the above purposes, and it was also made an offense to assist any man or men engaged in a strike. The courts were never backward in enforcing these statutes, but gradually, as the suffrage was extended, and the laboring classes came to have a voice and vote in matters of government, the old statutes were repealed and replaced by others less favorable to the employer.

The courts, however, both in England, and in this country, being far removed from popular control, have stubbornly contested every foot of the advance made by the working classes toward equality under the law. The history of this process through the centuries, interesting as it might be, is not involved in our present discussion, which is necessarily confined to those recent decisions, which go to make up or directly influence the existing body of the law on this subject. It is important to note, however, that in monarchial England, where the hard statutes against labor had their origin, and where the decisions of the courts necessarily reflected the harshness of the statutory law, all has been changed by recent legislation. While in this country, having borrowed from England the uncivilized and harsh principles of her early law, our courts have thus far been able to prevent anything like the sweeping changes in the law affecting laborers which has taken place in England. A familiar example of the progress of the English law relating to workmen is found in the celebrated Taff Vale case.[39] In that case a strike having arisen in August, 1900, among the employés of the Taff Vale Railway who were organized into a society, but not a corporation, it was decided by the House of Lords that an injunction would issue against the society and all its members, also that the society could be sued and the money in its treasury, collected to pay benefits to widows and orphans, could be used to pay any judgment for damages which the Railroad Company might recover as a result of the acts of the strikers. In the argument of this case, Haldane, K. C., pointed out for the Society, the danger of the rule which the Court in fact adopted. He said:[40]

"A trade union then is not a corporation nor an individual, nor a partnership. It is like a club, not a legal entity: and there are good reasons for this view. If the society can be sued as such, the funds intended for the benefit of widows and orphans can be reached and perhaps exhausted in consequence of improper and

39 Taff Vale Ry. Co. v. Amalgamated Society of Railway Servants, L. R. App. Cases, 1901, p. 426.

40 *Id.*, p. 435.

illegal acts of the society's officers. That would be a great calamity and was surely not intended by the Legislature."

The Court, however, decided in all respects in favor of the contentions of the Railway Company and issued an injunction against the society and its members forbidding picketing and interference with the railway company and its strike breakers, which reads very much like many of our own Federal Court injunctions issued in similar cases. Note now the difference between the action of the law-making branch of the English Government and our own in the same situation. The most we could hope to do with a decision like the Taff Vale case, and there are many of them in this country, would be slightly to lessen its hardship by statutes so harmless that the courts would permit them to stand. While in England, on the other hand, the Legislature being free to act for the best interests of the people, according to its own judgment, promptly passed a statute which cut up the Taff Vale decision by the roots and entirely revolutionized the law of England upon the subject.[41]

Section 5, Subdivision 3 of the Act provides:

"An act done by a person in contemplation or furtherance of a trade dispute shall not be actionable on the ground only that it induces some other person to break a contract of employment, or that it is an inter-

[41] Trade Disputes Act, 1906, Secs. 1–5.

ference with the trade, business or employment of some other person, or with the right of some other person, to dispose of his capital or his labor as he wills."

Section 5, Sub-Division 3 of the Act Provides:

"The expression 'trade dispute' means any dispute between employers and workmen or between workmen and workmen which is connected with the employment or non-employment or the terms of employment, or with the conditions of labor of any person, and the expression 'workmen' means all persons employed in trade or industry, whether or not in the employment of the employer with whom a trade dispute arises."

Speaking of the effect of this statute in a subsequent case [42] it is said:

"This appeal raises questions of difficulty and of general importance as to the meaning and effect of the Trade Disputes Act of 1906, and particularly of Sec. 3 of that act. It is plain that the main object of the act was to put trade unions in a peculiar and preferential position, and to treat trade disputes differently from all other disputes. Thus Sec. 1 alters the law of conspiracy — or rather, I should say, repeals the law of conspiracy — where there is a trade dispute, but leaves it intact in every other case. Sec. 2 sanctions peaceful picketing where there is trade dispute. Sec. 3 was probably intended as a rider to Sec. 1. It al-

[42] Conway v. Wade, L. R. Kings Bench Division, 1908, Vol. II, p. 844.

ters the established common law liability of an individual apart from conspiracy, not generally, but only where there is a trade dispute, either in contemplation or in existence."

That this statute is not popular with the English courts clearly appears from the case last cited,[43] and others.[44] But as the cases mentioned show, the courts feel bound to enforce it and give effect to its meaning, however shocking it seems to them. Now contrast this with the action of our own courts, in holding a statute unconstitutional and void because it forbade a Railway Company to discharge employés merely because they belonged to a labor union; [45] and in holding the Employers Liability Act void, providing that contributory negligence of the injured should not be a defense when it was slight and that of the employer was gross.[46]

While the decision last mentioned proceeds upon the ground that the act was not confined to subjects of interstate commerce and hence was not within the domain of congressional regulation, the State courts unhesitatingly destroy kindred legislation on the broad ground that it deprives the employer of his

43 Reversed 78 L. J. K. B. 1025.

44 Amalgamated Society of Railway Servants v. Osborne, L. R. App. Cases, 1910, p. 87; Markt v. Knight (1910), 2 K. B. 1021, 79 L. J. K. B. 939.

45 Adair v. U. S., 208 U. S. 161.

46 Employers' Liability cases, 207 U. S. 463.

property, without "due process of law" and is consequently void under the Fourteenth amendment to the Federal Constitution, as well as under most of the State Constitutions.[47]

These decisions and others like them bring into sharp relief the difficulty in this country of changing the old law affecting laborers and labor unions, so as to make it conform to public sentiment and to the intention of the law-making branch of the government. Precisely what part the decisions of our courts have thus far played in this movement remains to be considered.

One of the early Christian Kings of England,[48] introduced his criminal statutes with the following general, but very commendable language:

> "Though any one sin or deeply foredo himself, let the corrections be regulated so that it be becoming to God and tolerable before the world. And let him who has power of judgment very earnestly bear in mind what he himself desires when he says: 'forgive us our trespasses as we forgive those who trespass against us' and we command that Christian men on no account, for altogether too little, condemn to death; but rather let gentle punishment be decreed for the benefit of the people, and let not be destroyed for little, God's handiwork and his own purchase which he dearly bought."

47 Ives v. South Buffalo Ry. Co., 201 N. Y. 271; Durkin v. Kingston Coal Co., 171 Pa. St. 193.

48 Canute, 1017–35.

When the good king had finished his preamble and got down to the business at hand, he fixed the punishment of those who violated his statue, by providing, concerning the offender:

> "That his hands be cut off, or his feet, or both, according as the deed may be. And if he have wrought yet greater wrong, then let his eyes be put out, and his nose and his ears and his upper lip cut off and let him be scalped; whichever of these those shall counsel whose duty it is to counsel thereupon, so that punishment be inflicted and also the soul be preserved." [49]

I am always reminded of old King Canute and his criminal statutes, when I read the decisions of our courts relating to labor disputes. The decisions always abound with satisfying phrases about the "Dignity of Labor," "Sacredness of Contract," "The Right to Work" and the like, but when the decision gets down to the question presented in the particular case, and has finished with the Labor Organization before it, that unfortunate party is apt to bear a strong resemblance to one of King Canute's subjects after a collision with that Monarch's criminal law.

As we have previously seen, the year 1800 was ushered in, in England, by the passage of the statute [50] which practically forbade any combination

[49] *Stephen's History of the Criminal Law,* Vol. I, pp. 58, 59.
[50] 40 Geo. III, c. 60.

among laborers to obtain an advance of wages or to lessen the hours of work, and which also prohibited strikes and the giving of aid to strikers. This statute was continued in effect until 1824 when it was repealed and two other statutes were passed, one in 1824 and one in 1825, much less hostile to labor.[51] The act of 1825, contained no provisions which made men liable to summary punishment for promoting strikes. It is at this point that the courts take up the fight and by a series of decisions based upon what they are pleased to term the common law, practically maintain much of the hardship and injustice of the old statute which had been repealed.[52] The state of the law under these decisions is thus described by Sir James Fitzjames Stephen, a Justice of the Queen's Bench:[53]

"A bare agreement, not to work except upon certain specified terms, was, so long as this view of the law prevailed, all that the law permitted to workmen. If a single step was taken to dissuade systematically other persons from working, those who took it incurred the risk of being held to conspire to injure the employer, or to conspire to obstruct him in the conduct of his business. It is difficult to see how, in the case of a conflict of interests, it is possible to separate the two

[51] 6 Geo. IV, c. 129.

[52] These decisions are compiled in *Stephen's History of the Criminal Law of England*, Vol. III, p. 217.

[53] Stephen, Vol. III, p. 218.

objects of benefiting yourself and injuring your antagonist. Every strike is in the nature of an act of war. Gain on one side implies loss on the other; and to say that it is lawful to combine to protect your own interests, but unlawful to combine to injure your antagonist, is taking away with one hand a right given with the other."

These decisions reached their culmination when it was held in substance that the objects of a trade union were so far illegal that the embezzlement of its funds was not an offense against the statute.[54] From this point on, statute after statute was passed in England to correct the injustice of the Court decisions until, at the present time, as we have seen, there is little of the old law relating to labor organizations left in that country. The "common law" applied by the courts after the remedial statute of 1825 had been passed, seems to have been invented by the Judiciary in order to keep laborers and labor unions in subjection. This must be so, because the whole subject had been minutely regulated by statute and with the repeal of the statutes, the decisions of the courts based thereon must also have fallen.[55]

I have hastily sketched the development of the

54 Hornby v. Close, L. R. 2 Q. B. 153; Farrer v. Close, L. R. 4 Q. B. 602.

55 This whole subject is discussed in *Stephen's History of the Criminal Law of England*, by an authority who certainly was not friendly to trade unions, nor over critical of the courts. See Vol. III, pp. 203–27.

law of England on the subject under consideration, in part at least, because it is easier to see what the courts have done in another country, than it is to see what they are doing in our own. Every student of the subject must admit the hostility manifested by the English courts to laborers and labor unions, and their repeated attempts to maintain the principles of the old law, even though this involved disregarding the remedial statutes which were, from time to time passed. It is not always so easy for us, however, to admit the equally obvious truth that our own courts are engaged in doing identically the same thing.

Our courts early showed an inclination to apply the rules of the earliest English Law on the subject by forbidding laborers to continue their organization,[56] and by practically prohibiting strikes.[57] These decisions, have, of course, been modified in the particulars mentioned,[58] but the rules now existing are hardly less shocking in their injustice than those announced by the English courts early in the last century.

Compare the rules which the courts have devised for the government of the employer and employés in the contests constantly waged between organized labor and capital. The right of an employer to dis-

[56] 37 *Am. Law Review*, 431.

[57] Farmers' Loan & Trust Co. v. Northern Pac. R. R. Co., 60 Fed. 803, opinion by Jenkins, circuit judge.

[58] Arthur v. Oakes, 63 Fed. 310.

charge an employé at any time for any reason or for no reason and to give notice to other employers of such discharge and the reasons for it is well settled.[59]

Some years ago the Western Union Telegraph Company, having become aware that certain of its employés had joined a labor union, immediately discharged them without notice and without other cause and also notified other employers of such discharge and the reasons for it. *In other words, the discharged men were "Blacklisted."* The employés, having witnessed many successful applications to the courts by employers under similar circumstances applied to the Court themselves, setting up that the defendant company had unlawfully conspired with other parties mentioned to destroy the labor union and to work irreparable injury to the men, not only by discharging them, but by preventing their employment elsewhere. The Federal Court, however, in which the action was brought, turned a deaf ear to the complaint of the employés and laid down the rights of the employers in the following terms:[60]

"As in the absence of contract for employment for a definite period, the employer may discharge his employés at any time for any reason, or for no reason,

59 Boyer v. Western Union Telegraph Co., 124 Fed. 246; *The Modern Law of Labor Unions, by Martin,* Sec. 275 and cases cited.

60 124 Fed. 246.

there can be no such thing as an unlawful conspiracy to destroy a labor union by discharging its members or refusing to employ them. An employer, having discharged employés for belonging to a labor union, has the right to keep a book containing their names, and showing the reason of their discharge and to invite inspection thereof by other employers, even though the latter therefor refuse to hire the discharged employés."

and again:

"An allegation in a bill by members of a labor union for an injunction, that defendant, its officers and agents have unlawfully combined and confederated to destroy the union and by threats, intimidation and coercion, and otherwise, are interfering with plaintiffs and with others of their employés for uniting with the union, and are seeking to prevent those discharged from obtaining employment" states no cause of action.

Now the correlative rights which the employés should possess in order to be on even a substantial equality with the employers is to quit work at any time, for any cause, or for no cause, and in any number, and to publish to all other employés the reason for such action. That employés do not possess these rights and that they are constantly being severely punished and even imprisoned for attempting to perform such acts is well known. The courts divide strikes into two classes,— lawful and unlawful. Strikes are declared unlawful sometimes because of their object, and sometimes because of the means employed. No one can tell in advance what a court will hold, for there is no uniformity in the rulings. The view-point, whim, or caprice of a judge determines, in the majority of cases, whether a strike, which means almost life or death to thousands of employés, will be permitted as lawful, or enjoined and broken up by the courts as unlawful. For example,— a sympathetic strike on the part of railroad employés in order to aid the striking employés of the Pullman Palace Car Company was held to be unlawful [61] and the organization of the railway employés for such purpose a conspiracy for which various of them served long terms in prison. In the Thomas case just cited, Mr. Justice Taft said:

"All the employés had the right to quit their employment."

Having, like King Canute conceded that much for Christian charity, the learned Justice proceeds:

"But they had no right to combine to quit, in order thereby to compel their employer to withdraw from a mutually profitable relation with a third person for the purpose of injuring that third person, when the relation thus sought to be broken had no effect whatever on the character or reward of their services. It is the motive for quitting and the end sought thereby that make the injury inflicted unlawful and the combination by which it is effected unlawful conspiracy."

61 Thomas v. Cincinnati, etc., Ry. Co., 62 Fed. 803, opinion by Taft, J. *in re* Debs, 158 U. S. 564.

So also it is an "indictable conspiracy" for employés to combine and notify their employer that unless he discharges certain named persons, they will strike.[62] In the case last mentioned, nothing more was shown than that the employés notified the employer that unless certain men were discharged they would quit. Of this act, the Court said:

> "This was an unwarrantable interference with the conduct of his (the employer's) business, and it seems impossible that such acts should not be in their usual effects highly injurious. . . . I cannot regard such a course of conduct as lawful. It is no answer to the above considerations to say that the employer is not compelled to submit to the demand of his employés; that the penalty of refusal is simply that they will leave his service. There is this coercion:—The men agree to leave simultaneously in large numbers and by preconcerted action. We cannot close our eyes to the fact, that the threat of the workman to quit the employer, under these circumstances, is equivalent to a threat that unless he yield to their unjustifiable demand, they will derange his business and thus cast a heavy loss upon him. . . . In such a condition of affairs it is idle to suggest that the manufacturer is free to reject the terms which the confederates offer."

Contrast this rule with the employer's right to discharge an employé for any reason, or for no reason.

So also it is held that a strike by the members

[62] State v. Donaldson, 32 N. J. Law, 151.

of a labor union because an employer has, as the union finds, unjustly discharged an employé, and refuses to take him back, is unlawful, and will be enjoined.[63]

Aside from holding strikes unlawful, because of their object, a favorite practice of the courts is to declare them unlawful because of the means employed. Since no possible good can come to strikers if their places can be immediately filled by other employés, it becomes necessary for them to inform those about to take their places, of the existence of the strike and the reason for it. This object is best accomplished by the strikers or their friends remaining in the vicinity of the work, and meeting the new men as they arrive and persuading them not to accept employment. This is called "picketing." A recent decision of the Illinois Supreme Court is to the effect that picketing for the purpose merely of peaceably dissuading from going to work, the men who were brought in by the company to take the strikers' places, was unlawful and would be enjoined.[64] While some courts say that picketing without violence is permissible, yet as it is always possible for the employer to incite some one to violence, and in many cases individual employés will resort to violence, it easily happens that some disorder attends

[63] Reynolds v. Davis, 198 Mass. 294.

[64] Barnes v. Typographical Union, 232 Ill. 424.

upon picketing, and since the courts uniformly hold this a sufficient reason for granting an injunction, it has come about that striking employés have practically been deprived by the decisions of the courts of the right to peaceably dissuade others from taking their places.[65] A pertinent inquiry of the labor organizations at this point is, why not depend upon the criminal law in the case of a strike as in all other cases, to punish any breach of the peace or other violence? Proceeding under the form of the criminal law insures a jury trial, and proof of guilt beyond a reasonable doubt, before one charged with an offense can be punished. Why should a court of equity dispense with all these safeguards and proceed summarily to imprison men without a jury trial, and upon evidence which would never sustain a conviction in a criminal action?

The use of the injunctive process by the courts in this class of cases has become so common in recent years that we have coined, to describe it, the expression "government by injunction." The exercise of this power by the courts has been of such a char-

[65] State v. Stockford, 77 Conn. 227; N. Y. Central Iron Works v. Brennan, 105 Supp. (N. Y.), 865; Schwarcz v. International L. G. W. Union, 68 Misc. (N. Y.), 529; Curran v. Galen, 152 N. Y. 33; U. S. v. Kane, 23 Fed. 748; Frank v. Denver, etc., Ry., 23 Fed. 757; Casey v. Typographical Union, 45 Fed. 135; Martin on the Law of Labor Unions (1910), Secs. 168–9.

acter as to alarm even the most conservative members of the legal profession.[66]

Another method resorted to by labor to enforce its demands against employers is the "boycott." This term has been variously defined, but in a general sense it means the refusal of the employés engaged in a trade dispute to patronize the employer with whom such dispute exists and also to procure as many sympathizers and as large a portion of the public as possible, also to withhold patronage from the objectionable employer. This latter action is usually referred to as a "Secondary Boycott." It is to the members of the labor organization what the "Blacklist" is to the employer. By the "Blacklist," the employer gives out information in order to prevent the employment of certain laborers. The laborers, when they publish an employer as "unfair," give out information intended to prevent various persons from patronizing such employer. Note, however, that while the "Blacklist" is uniformly upheld by the courts, except as it has been prohibited by Legislative action, the "Secondary Boycott," so-called, is as uniformly condemned and prohibited.[67] These de-

[66] 11 *Harvard Law Review*, p. 487, article by Charles Noble Gregory, Dean of the Law School of Iowa University. Also, 42 *American Law Review*, p. 161 and p. 200.

[67] Thomas v. Cincinnati, etc., Ry., 62 Fed., p. 803 and cases there cited by Mr. Justice Taft; Hopkins v. Oxley Stave Co., 83 Fed. 912; Gompers, Mitchell and Morrison, petitioners, v. Bucks Stove & Range Co., decided by the Supreme Court of

cisions show that when, by the "Blacklist," an employer is able to break up a labor union and starve the employés and their families into submission, no cause of action arises, and the laborer is without remedy. But, when by publishing an employer as "unfair" a loss of business is caused, such act is said to work "irreparable damage" to the employer and all the machinery of the courts is set in motion to prevent it. In the Gompers case just referred to, which is the latest utterance of our highest Court, on this subject, it is said:

"The Court's protective and restraining powers extend to every device whereby *property* is irreparably damaged or commerce is illegally restrained. . . . In case of an unlawful conspiracy (agreeing to publish certain employers as unfair) the agreement to act in concert when the signal is published, gives the words Unfair, We don't patronize, or similar expressions, a force not inhering in the words themselves, and therefore exceeding any possible right of speech which a single individual might have. Under such circumstances they have become what have been called "verbal acts," and as much subject to injunction as the use of any other force whereby property is unlawfully damaged." [68]

the United States May 15, 1911, 221 U. S. 418, and cases there cited.

[68] While the Supreme Court, by disposing of the case on a question of procedure, avoided the necessity of confirming the sentences of imprisonment which had been imposed on the labor leaders, Gompers, Mitchell, and Morrison, the language

When a court is at liberty, as this decision plainly shows all courts are in cases of trade disputes, to treat words as acts, it is only a step to treat acts as words, and all principles of law by which men's conduct has heretofore been judged will vanish, and in its place we will have simply the uncontrollable discretion of a judge.

The United States Circuit Court of Appeals, for the Southern District of New York, in Paine Lumber Company et al. v. Neal et al., decided November 29th, 1911, on appeal from an order granting a preliminary injunction, has carried the doctrine of enjoining strikes to its logical conclusion. In that case it appears that the complainants were manufacturers of doors, frames, and other varieties of wood-work. The defendants included officers and members of the United Brotherhood of Carpenters and Joiners of America. A dispute having arisen, the complainants, who conducted an "open shop," sought an injunction, restraining the defendants from agreeing to refuse to handle materials produced by complainants and from publishing the complainants' products as "unfair," and from attempting to induce any person, to either decline employment with complainants or to quit their employ, and also for various other purposes. An injunction was granted which enjoined the defendants, among other things,

quoted makes it plain that the court is tenaciously holding on to all the power heretofore asserted in this class of cases.

"from interfering in any manner, with . . . the installation or setting up of any of the products of the complainants and from . . . communicating . . . to any other person, firm, or corporation, any statement or notice of any kind, or character, whatsoever, calling attention to the fact that your complainants, or their business or their products are or were or have been declared unfair, or on any unfair list, or that your complainants should not be patronized with or dealt with or their products purchased, used, handled, worked upon, or dealt in, because made in an open or non-union shop, and from . . . attempting to induce any person or persons whomsoever, to decline employment or cease employment, or not to seek employment with any person, firm or corporation because such person, firm or corporation may have made contracts or proposed to make contracts, with complainants . . . and from requesting customers or those who might become customers of the complainants, to purchase their wood materials from, or have their wood-work done by persons or corporations who use the union label of the United Brotherhood of Carpenters and Joiners of America, . . . so that they may avoid labor troubles."

The opinion in this case by Mr. Justice Coxe was filed May 22nd, 1911, and the injunctional order from which the above quotations are made was filed May 9th, 1911. Neither the opinion nor the injunctional order appears in the Federal Reporter covering the time of the decision. The Circuit Court of Appeals affirmed the order on November 20th, 1911, in an opinion which gives no idea of the sweeping nature of the injunction granted.

To the credit of the Judiciary, it is to be said that the present monstrously unjust state of the law on this subject was not built up, without powerful protests from some of the Judges. Lack of space will permit me to refer to only one of these,— that of Judge Caldwell, in his dissenting opinion in the Oxley Stave Co. case above noticed, where he vigorously protested against the injunction issued by the Court prohibiting an orderly boycott. Among other things, he said: [69]

"This proposition, that it is unlawful for men to do collectively what they may do, without wrong, individually, was enunciated more than a century and a half ago, when all manner of association and coöperation, among men, offensive to the king, or not in the interest of despotic power or the ruling classes, or not approved by the judges were declared by the courts to be criminal conspiracies. It was promulgated at a time . . . when laborers had no rights their employers or the courts were bound to respect. The idea of the power of men in association has always been abhorrent to despots, and to those who wish to oppress their fellow men, because its free exercise is fatal to despotism and oppression. The strength it imparts carries its own protection. In all ages those who seek to deprive the people of their rights justify their action by ancient and

[69] 83 Fed., p. 930.

obsolete precedents, and by coining definitions suited to their ends. In 'that codeless myriad of precedent,' running back to the Dark Ages called the 'Common Law,' it is not difficult to find a precedent for inflicting any injustice or oppression on the common people. But these precedents, so shocking to our sense of right, so inimical to our constitution and social and economic conditions, and so subversive of the liberty of men, should be permitted to sleep in profound oblivion. They neither justify nor palliate encroachments on the natural and constitutional rights of the citizens. . . . What each individual member of a labor organization may lawfully do, acting singly, becomes (under the rule adopted in that case) an unlawful conspiracy when done by them collectively. Singly, they may boycott; collectively, they cannot. The individual boycott is lawful, because it can accomplish little or nothing. The collective boycott is unlawful because it might accomplish something. People can only free themselves from oppression by organized force. No people could gain or maintain their rights or liberties, acting singly, and any class of citizens in the state subject to unjust burdens or oppression can only gain relief by combined action. . . . It was the recognition of these truths that prompted the promulgation of the proposition we are discussing. The doctrine (announced by the majority of the court) compels every man to be a stranger in action to every other man. It is a doctrine abhorrent to freemen. It is in hostility to a law of man's nature, which prompts him to associate with his fellows for his protection, defense, and improvement. Under its operation every religious, political, or social organization in the country may be enjoined from combined action, if their religious faith or political creed or practice is *obnoxious* to the judge. It was originally designed for this very purpose."

On a subsequent page, the same learned justice said:

"While laborers, by the application to them of the doctrine we are considering, are reduced to individual action, it is not so with the forces arrayed against them. A corporation is an association of individuals for combined action; trusts are corporations combined together for the very purpose of collective action and boycotting; and capital, which is the product of labor, is in itself a powerful collective force. . . . What is 'competition' when done by capital is 'conspiracy' when done by the laborers. No amount of verbal dexterity can conceal or justify this glaring discrimination."

In discussing the decisions of the courts relating to industrial disputes, I cannot, of course, refer to all the cases on the subject. I have not referred to the sailors' case,[70] wherein it is held that the constitutional prohibition against "slavery" and "involuntary servitude" does not apply to sailors and that this class of laborers *may still be held to involuntary servitude.* I have not stopped to call attention to the inconsistency between the decision in the Debs case,[71] wherein it is held that the control

[70] Robertson v. Baldwin, 165 U. S. 275.

[71] 158 U. S. 564.

of Congress over Interstate Commerce is so complete that it may regulate the conduct of the employés engaged therein to the extent of enjoining them from going on a sympathetic strike, and the decision in the Adair case,[72] wherein it is held that Congress has so little power over the conduct of those engaged in Interstate Commerce that it cannot lawfully forbid *employers* engaged therein discharging employés, merely because of the employés' membership in a labor union. Neither have I dealt with the cases permitting laborers to be kidnapped in order that they might be placed on trial in localities where they could not have lawfully been taken for trial.[73] These cases and others like them have aroused great bitterness on the part of the working classes against the courts and have been thoroughly discussed in the labor and radical press of the country. The dissenting opinions in the Pettibone, Robertson and Adair cases certainly show that there is some foundation for the hostile criticism which has been leveled at the Court's acts in these and kindred cases.

I have simply tried to gather together, on this branch of the discussion, sufficient of the decisions to

72 208 U. S. 161.

73 Pettibone v. Nichols, 203 U. S. 192. See also, U. S. v. Rauscher, 119 U. S. 419; Hyatt v. Corkran, 188 U. S. 691; Munsey v. Clough, 196 U. S. 364; Warren v. U. S., 183 Fed. 718. Also, hearings May 27 and 29, 1911, on House Resolution No. 6, published in pamphlet form, relating to the extradition of John J. McNamara.

show the general and well settled rules of law which the courts have devised in this country to govern trade disputes between capital and organized labor. These rules speak for themselves. The restrictions they place upon labor have been recently summarized by an able law writer as follows:[74]

"They (employés) are not permitted to strike to compel men to join the Union. They are not permitted, in even a lawful strike, to employ pickets to persuade men not to take employment as strike breakers, nor to maintain banners before an establishment giving notice of a strike in progress there. They are not permitted to enter upon a merely sympathetic strike against employers with whom they have no trade dispute, and a strike to secure to the Union the right to pass upon grievances between individual members and their employers is considered a sympathetic strike. They are not permitted to exact by strike the payment of a penalty by an employer for violation of Union regulations. They will not be accorded judicial aid, either as organizations or as individuals, to prevent blacklisting by a combination of employers."

While the foregoing was intended as a summation of the law of Massachusetts on the subject, it practically states the law of the whole country on the subject as well, and is certainly as liberal to the employés as the rules laid down by the Federal Courts.

[74] "Labor questions in the Courts of Massachusetts," by Arthur March Brown, 42 *Am. Law Review*, 706, p. 733.

Turn now to the statement of what the *employer* may do, and you read that he has an unrestricted right to discharge, to blacklist and to lock out his employés, and that the injunctive process of our courts with its arbitrary and despotic power to punish and imprison without a jury trial, is always at his command.[75]

Just as the English judges of the last century seemed incapable of understanding that the "Statute of Laborers" had been repealed and that the day of individual contract between employer and employed had arrived, so our judges seem unable to grasp the idea that individual contract between employer and employed has been superseded by collective action. The English judges, however, could offer but feeble opposition to the advance of the new order, for the Legislative branch of that government was supreme, and its laws were as binding upon the judges as upon the humblest individual in the land. With us, however, the case is different. The judges have assumed a power which makes their will superior to the popular will. They have raised the issue, whether the will of the people or the opinions of judges shall constitute the supreme law of the land.

Turning now to the class of cases which deal with "property interests" and "vested rights" we find

[75] "The Rationale of the Injunction," by Wm. Trickett, Dean of Dickinson's School of Law, Carlisle, Pa., 42 *Am. Law Review.*

no lack of initiative and enterprise on the part of the courts in protecting and advancing such rights. If our courts have been reactionary where the rights of the individual were concerned, they certainly have been progressive where the rights of property were involved. We hear much in these days of the dangers arising from great wealth and of the menace special privilege is to our institutions. We seldom stop to think that the twin pillars upon which the whole structure of special privilege rests in this country, are two decisions of the Supreme Court of the United States.

In 1795 the Legislature of Georgia sold about 500,000 acres of public land belonging to that State to various parties and it was subsequently claimed that the legislators had been unduly and corruptly influenced to make the sale by the purchasers of the land. At any rate, the Legislature, as soon as it assembled the succeeding year, immediately passed an Act to rescind the sale of the year before, setting forth in great detail the fraud and bribery by which the sale had been effected. Thereafter, an action was brought, apparently collusive in character, by one Fletcher, against the defendant Peck, from whom Fletcher purchased certain of the lands in question, and Peck, in his turn derived title from the original purchasers.[76] Concerning the collusive character of the action and its apparent purpose not to settle any

[76] Fletcher v. Peck, 6 Cranch, 87.

real controversy, but to establish the validity of the titles procured through the fraudulent purchase, the Chief Justice, in his opinion, said:

"I have been very unwilling to proceed to the decision of this cause at all. It appears to me to bear strong evidence upon the face of it of being a mere feigned case. It is our duty to decide on the rights, but not on the speculations of parties."

Nevertheless, the Court lent itself to the purpose of the suit and decided the case. It would have been sufficient for the decision, of course, to hold, if such was the fact, that the defendant, Peck, was an innocent purchaser of the lands from those who acquired them originally of the State, and let the decision stop at that point. Either there was some doubt in the Court's mind as to the innocent character of Peck's purchase from the others, or for some other reason the Court thought it necessary to go further and discuss the question of how far, if at all, grants by the Legislature of a State, procured by bribery, could be inquired into. In the opinion, the Chief Justice says:

"That corruption should find its way into the governments of our infant republics, and contaminate the very source of legislation, or that impure motives should contribute to the passage of a law, or the formation of a legislative contract, are circumstances most deeply to be deplored. . . . It may well be doubted how far the validity of a law depends upon the motives of its framers, and how far the particular inducements, operating on members of the supreme sovereign power of a state, to the formation of a contract by that power, are examinable in a court of justice. If the principle be conceded, that an act of the supreme sovereign power might be declared null by a court, in consequence of the means which procured it, still would there be much difficulty in saying to what extent those means must be applied to produce this effect. Must it be direct corruption, or would interest or undue influence of any kind be sufficient? Must the vitiating cause operate on a majority, or on what number of the members? Would the act be null, whatever might be the wish of the nation, or would its obligation or nullity depend upon the public sentiment? If the majority of the legislature be corrupted, it may well be doubted, whether it be within the province of the judiciary to control their conduct and, if less than a majority act from impure motives, the principles by which judicial interference would be regulated, is not clearly discerned."

The suggestions of the Chief Justice, concerning the inability of a Court to grant relief against the corrupt grants of the Legislatures, were seized upon by the courts, and the rule which he suggested, speedily became the settled law.[77] In an early case wherein a railroad company had bought valuable

[77] *Cooley Constitutional Limitations,* 7th Edition, p. 257, and cases cited.

privileges from a Legislature, the Court, when applied to by the public for relief, said: [78]

"Official morality in us requires that we shall not assume the authority to judge of the official morality of the Legislature. For the faithfulness and honesty of their public acts, we repeat, they are responsible to the people alone and not by means of a trial before the courts."

This doctrine soon came to be applied to the acts of boards of aldermen and municipal legislatures generally. Concerning the motives of the members of the Board of Supervisors of San Francisco in passing an ordinance alleged to have been improperly secured, the Supreme Court of the United States recently said: [79]

"Their motives, considered as the moral inducement for their votes, will vary with the different members of the legislative body. The divers character of such motives and the impossibility of penetrating into the hearts of men and ascertaining the truth, precludes all such inquiries as impracticable."

Thus, through the mere dictum of the Court in the collusive action of Fletcher v. Peck, has the law become established that the bribery and corruption by which any grant or valuable right is obtained

[78] Sunbury & Erie R. R. Co. v. Cooper, 33 Pa. St. 278.
[79] Soon Hing v. Crowley, 113 U. S. 703–11.

from a Legislature, national, state or municipal, will not be examined into by a Court for the purpose of relieving against the fraudulent or corrupt transaction. The official morality of the judges, so they say, will not permit them to inquire into the official morality of the members of the Legislatures. This, of course, was a tremendous gain for what is termed property rights and vested interests, but there was still the possibility that a succeeding Legislature would rescind the corrupt act of its predecessors and thereby destroy the value of that which had been corruptly obtained.

As the courts declared that for every corrupt act, Legislators were responsible to the public alone, the public was certain speedily to replace the unworthy legislators with worthy ones, and the latter might protect the public interests by repealing the grants which had been corruptly made.

Another case soon arose, however, in which a doctrine was announced which closed this door of hope to the public.[80] That case arose out of a sordid contest, semi-political and semi-religious in character, among the Trustees of Dartmouth College to obtain control of that institution.

The brief account here given of the facts leading up to the Dartmouth College decision, is condensed from the historical discussion of that case by Jesse

80 Trustees of Dartmouth College v. Woodward, 4 Wheaton, 517.

F. Orton, in his pamphlet, "The Confusion of Property with Privilege," published in 1909 by the Committee to Inquire into the Status of Democracy.

Dartmouth College was founded in 1769 by virtue of a charter by the then Governor of New Hampshire in the name, of course, of the English King. The charter provided for the government of the institution by twelve trustees. The first President, Eleazer Wheelock, who was named in the charter and was given the privilege of appointing his successor, died in 1779, having appointed his son, John Wheelock, to succeed him.

About the year 1800, two factions in the Board of Trustees arose. One was headed by President Wheelock, who was a Presbyterian, while his opponents in the Board were Congregationalists.

After a while the struggle took on a political tinge, and the faction of President Wheelock became identified with the anti-Federalists and the other faction was strongly Federal. While the Federalists were in control of the State, the Board of Trustees assumed to remove President Wheelock from office.

The anti-Federalists in 1816, elected William Plumer to the office of Governor and the new Governor and the Legislature passed acts amending the college charter, the principal effect being to increase the number of trustees from twelve to twenty-one, and Wheelock was restored to the position of President of the College. The old anti-Wheelock Trustees refused to take part in the reorganization of the college, and finally brought an action against Woodward, secretary and treasurer of the corporation, as it was reorganized, under the new Board of Trustees, to recover the corporate books and other corporate records.

The Supreme Court of New Hampshire decided the case against the Trustees and in favor of the Wheelock, anti-Federal and Presbyterian faction.[81]

Daniel Webster, a graduate of the college, had been retained by President Wheelock, sometime before the passage of the act increasing the Board of Directors, but when the litigation began, was induced to abandon Wheelock and espouse the cause of the Federalist faction of the Board. See *Life of Webster* by Henry Cabot Lodge.[82] In this work, Mr. Lodge says:

"Mr. Webster was fully aware that he could rely, in any aspect of the case, upon the sympathy of Marshall and Washington (Associate Justice Bushrod Washington). He was equally certain of the unyielding opposition of Duvall and Todd; the other three judges, Johnson, Livingston and Story, were known to be adverse to the college, but were possible converts. The first point was to increase the sympathy of the Chief Justice to an eager and even passionate support. Mr. Webster knew the chord to strike, and he touched it with a mas-

[81] Report of this case is re-printed with arguments of counsel, 65 N. H. 473.

[82] "Life of Webster" in *American Statesman Series*, p. 1.

ter hand. This was the 'something left out,' of which we know the general drift, and we can easily imagine the effect."

Mr. Webster in publishing his argument in this case always admitted that there was "something left out" and it is this expression to which Mr. Lodge referred in the above quotation.

Further referring to the manner in which Mr. Webster played upon the prejudices of the Chief Justice, because of his intense Federalism, Mr. Lodge says:[83]

"In the midst of all the legal and constitutional arguments, relevant and irrelevant, even in the pathetic appeal which he used so well in behalf of his alma mater, Mr. Webster boldly and yet skillfully introduced the political view of the case. So delicately did he do it that an attentive listener did not realize that he was straying from the field of 'mere reason' into that of political passion. Here no man could equal him or help him, for here his eloquence had full scope, and on this he relied to arouse Marshall, whom he thoroughly understood. In occasional sentences he pictured his beloved college under the wise rule of Federalists and the church. He depicted the party assault that was made upon her. He showed the citadel of learning threatened with unholy invasion and falling helplessly into the hands of Jacobins and free-thinkers."

[83] *Id.*, p. 88.

Mr. Lodge shows that the point upon which the case was actually decided, namely that a charter was a contract and consequently that under the Constitution, no law could be passed which impaired it, was really suggested to Mr. Webster by one of the trustees, who was not a lawyer, and that Mr. Webster thought little of the point and devoted but small space to it in the argument and in his brief.[84] He seems to have depended more upon other legal points, but particularly he sought to inflame the passions of the Chief Justice and arouse his well known hostility to Jefferson.

Of course the Jacobins mentioned by Webster in his argument were the followers of Jefferson and the free-thinkers were Governor Plumer and his supporters, who were then carrying on a struggle for equality of religious denominations in New Hampshire.

Mr. Lodge gives this further description of Mr. Webster's argument:

"As the tide of his resistless and solemn eloquence, mingled with his masterly argument, flowed on, we can imagine how the great Chief Justice roused like an old warhorse at the sound of the trumpet. The words of the speaker carried him back to early years of the century, when, in the full flush of manhood, at the head of his court, the last stronghold of Federalism, the last

[84] See also, *Dartmouth College Case Causes*, by John M. Shirley.

bulwark of sound government, he had faced the power of the triumphant Democrats. Once more it was Marshall against Jefferson — the judge against the president. Then he had preserved the ark of the Constitution. Then he had seen the angry waves of popular feeling breaking vainly at his feet. Now, in his old age, the conflict was revived. Jacobinism was raising its sacrilegious hand against the temples of learning, against the friends of order and good government. The joy of battle must have glowed once more in the old man's breast as he grasped anew his weapons and prepared with all the force of his indomitable will to raise yet another constitutional barrier across the path of his ancient enemies."

But after all had been said and done, the Court, Mr. Lodge concludes, was five to two against Mr. Webster and the old Board of Trustees. The Chief Justice, however, succeeded in preventing a decision and the Court adjourned for the term. Then began a campaign to "get at," to use the expression of Mr. Lodge, enough of the other judges so that uniting with the Chief Justice, they might constitute a majority. Mr. Shirley, in his work already cited, gives an excellent account of this process, and tells us how the judges were seen by personal and political friends and how certain pamphlets and arguments were sent to some and not to others, although the case had been closed and taken under advisement. Mr. Lodge says:

"The whole business was managed like a quiet, decorous political campaign."

Chancellor Kent, himself an intense Federalist, was brought into the matter, and his influence was brought to bear upon some of the judges of the Supreme Court.

Without going further into the details of this unpleasant transaction, suffice it for our purposes, that the work of influencing the judges was well done, and finally resulted in bringing all of them, except two, into agreement with the Chief Justice.

The case was then decided. The Federalists had gained a signal political victory. More than all, however, the doctrine had been declared that every charter, franchise, and privilege, such as exemption from taxation, and the like, which any corporation could secure from a legislature, was a contract and could not be in any way impaired by subsequent legislative action.

Couple with this proposition the further one originating in Fletcher v. Peck, that however fraudulent the means by which such franchise, charter or privilege was acquired, the court was powerless to give relief because of the fraud, and you have the foundation upon which our colossal fortunes rest, which grow out of special privilege.

Fletcher v. Peck made bribery of legislatures safe for the great interests engaged in it, and the Dartmouth College case made it profitable.

The occasional conviction of a petty legislative bribe taker or bribe giver, always the agent of some one higher up, is usually made the occasion for the Court to lecture the convicted party upon the serious nature of this offense. The Court is properly indignant at such an offense, but it must always be remembered that without the decisions I have mentioned, and the body of law built thereon, bribery of legislatures would be practically unknown, for it would be neither safe nor profitable to those great interests which usually suggest the crime, and always profit by it.

Chancellor Kent, speaking approvingly of the Dartmouth College case, shortly after its rendition, said:

"The decision in that case did more than any other single act proceeding from the authority of the United States, to throw an impregnable barrier around all rights and franchises derived from the grant of government."[85]

Some fifty years later, Mr. Justice Cole, of the Iowa Supreme Court, said:

"The practical effect of the Dartmouth College decision is to exalt the rights of the few above those of the many. And it is doubtless true that under the authority of that decision, more monopolies have been created and perpetuated and more wrongs and outrages upon the

[85] 1 Kent. Comm. 419.

people effected, than by any other single instrumentality in the government." [86]

A little later, that greatest of Constitutional Lawyers, Judge Cooley, said:

"It is under the protection of the decision in the Dartmouth College case that the most enormous and threatening powers in our country have been created; some of the great and wealthy corporations actually having greater influence in the country at large, and upon the legislation of the country, than the states to which they owe their corporate existence. Every privilege granted or right conferred — no matter by what means or on what pretense — being made inviolable by the constitution, the government is frequently found stripped of its authority in very important particulars by unwise, careless and corrupt legislation; and a clause of the federal constitution whose purpose was to preclude the repudiation of debts and just contracts, protects and perpetuates the evil. To guard against such calamities in the future, it is customary now for the people in forming their constitutions, to forbid the granting of corporate powers, except subject to amendment and repeal, but the improvident grants of an early day are beyond their reach." [87]

If a charter is a contract, then it would seem that every charter procured by fraud must be voidable, for nothing is better settled in the law than that

[86] Dubuque v. Railroad Co., 39 Iowa, 95, 96.
[87] *Cooley Constitutional Limitations*, 279–80 n.

fraud vitiates every contract. Under the rule of Fletcher v. Peck, however, a charter cannot be invalidated because it was procured by fraud, no matter how gross or open the fraud may be. The states organized after the Dartmouth College decision, were able, as Judge Cooley says, to guard themselves against the consequences of that decision by providing in their constitutions against the granting of corporate powers, except as they were subject to amendment and repeal. Then followed the Fourteenth Amendment to the Constitution, designed for the protection of the recently freed slaves, providing in substance that no State should deprive "any person of life, liberty or property without due process of law" or "deny to any person within its jurisdiction the equal protection of the laws." This provision was immediately seized upon by the courts and made to include corporations, and thereby grants and franchises to corporations have been rendered more valuable even than under the authority of the Dartmouth College decision.

CHAPTER VI

DANGERS OF THE POPULAR DISTRUST OF THE COURTS

THE judiciary is constitutionally the weakest department of the government. John Jay, the first Chief Justice of the Supreme Court of the United States, resigned because the Court had so little power, under the Constitution, that he felt it a waste of time to remain in that office. He was tendered a reappointment by President Adams in 1800, but declined it, saying:

"I left the Bench perfectly convinced that, under a system so defective, it would not obtain the energy, weight and dignity which was essential to its affording due support to the national government; nor acquire public confidence and respect which, as the last resort of the justice of the nation, it should possess. Hence, I am induced to doubt both the expediency and propriety of my returning to the Bench under the present system."[1]

The executive, with its command of the military forces, and Congress, with its control of the revenues, and each with an army of dependent appointees,

[1] Pellew, *Life of Jay*, pp. 337–8.

have the means at hand for the enforcement of their respective policies. The Judiciary has no such power. Judges do not even appoint the officers who execute their decrees. If a United States marshall should decline to execute the decree of a Federal Court, what could the Court do about it? The marshal is appointed by the President and is responsible to the President, and if the latter directs that the particular decree shall not be enforced, and the people support the President, that ends it. If a sheriff declines to execute the mandate of a State Court, the Court is powerless. The sheriff is elected by the people of a county, and is usually removable by the governor of the State. If the people and the governor support the sheriff in his refusal to execute the order of the court, the order will remain unexecuted and will accomplish nothing.

Without the confidence, approval and support of the people, all the opinions, decrees and judgments of the courts are only waste paper. While judges, and particularly federal judges, are farther removed from popular control than any other public officials, the enforcement of their orders and judgments depends wholly upon the confidence and good will of the people. At this point lies the danger! Independent of the popular will in the tenure of their office, but wholly dependent upon it for the enforcement of their judgments, the judges are constantly tempted to a conflict, in which they must always be worsted; and sometimes at great cost to the country.

Without dwelling upon the controversies between the courts and President Jefferson, or the later ones waged between the courts and President Jackson, I call attention only to two or three instances in later years where the opinions of the courts have been left without support in public sentiment. The Dred Scott case is a familiar example.[2] This case was brought by Dred Scott, a former slave, to secure his freedom because he had been taken into territory where slavery did not exist. The case came up to the Supreme Court of the United States, from the District of Missouri. The Court held that Dred Scott was not a citizen of Missouri and

> "not entitled as such to sue in its courts, and consequently that the Circuit Court had no jurisdiction of the case."[3]

This was all that it was necessary to decide, but the Court, hoping to shape the political policy of the country on the subject, and to lay down a rule to govern other cases, went further and held in effect that the Missouri Compromise was unconstitutional, and that Congress could not prohibit slavery in the territories.[4] This decision is, therefore, strikingly

[2] Dred Scott v. Sandford, 19 Howard, 393.

[3] *Id.*, p. 427.

[4] *Id.*, pp. 447–54.

like the recent decisions in the Standard Oil and Tobacco cases. In these cases last mentioned, all that it was necessary to hold was that the acts under consideration violated the Anti-Trust law, but the Court went further, and hoping to shape the political policy of the country on the subject according to its own economic theory, and in order to establish a rule to apply in other cases, held that *only* certain acts, which the Court in the future might characterize as "undue" restraints of trade, would violate the statute. In his debate with Lincoln, half a century ago, Judge Douglas speaking of the Dred Scott decision, well expressed the views, then and now, of those who argue that the decision of a Court of last resort is final. He said:

> "As a lawyer, I feel at liberty to appear before the Court and controvert any principle of law while the question is pending before the tribunal; but when the decision is made, my private opinion, your opinion, all other opinions must yield to the majesty of that authoritative adjudication. I have no idea of appealing from the decision of the Supreme Court upon a constitutional question, to the decisions of a tumultuous town meeting. . . . I respect the decisions of that august tribunal; I shall always bow in deference to them." [5]

Mr. Lincoln represented and stated the opposite view many times, and in various forms. He said:

[5] *Lincoln and Douglas Debates*, p. 16.

"I have expressed heretofore, and I now repeat, my opposition to the Dred Scott decision. . . . If I wanted to take Dred Scott from his master, I would be interfering with property, and that terrible difficulty that Judge Douglas speaks of, interfering with property, would arise. But I am doing no such thing as that; all that I am doing is refusing to obey it as a political rule. . . . Judge Douglas said last night that before the decision he might advance his opinion, and it might be contrary to the decision when it was made; but after it was made, he would abide by it until it was reversed. Just so! We let this property abide by the decision, but we will try to reverse that decision. We will try to put it where Judge Douglas would not object, for he says he will obey it until it is reversed. Somebody has to reverse that decision, since it is made; and we mean to reverse it, and we mean to do it peaceably."[6]

Unfortunately all the people were not as wise, nor as temperate as Mr. Lincoln. The decision was reversed, *but it was not reversed "peaceably."* An illustration of a more peaceful, but quite as effective a method of setting aside a judgment of the Supreme Court of the United States was given in 1859 by the State of Wisconsin.[7] In that case, the Federal Courts undertook to punish a man named Booth, because he had assisted a fugitive slave to escape. The

[6] From a speech delivered by Mr. Lincoln at Chicago, Ill., July 10, 1858.

[7] Ableman v. Booth, 11 Wis. 498.

Wisconsin officials, acting under the direction of the Supreme Court of the State, simply set Booth at liberty, and though the Supreme Court of the United States repeatedly and very solemnly reversed the decision of the Supreme Court of Wisconsin,[8] no one paid any attention to it, and Booth obtained his liberty.[9]

The legal tender cases [10] illustrate how, by the addition of Republican Judges to a Democratic Supreme Court, an unconstitutional law was converted into a constitutional one. In 1862 Congress had passed a law which made United States notes legal tender in payment of all debts, whether public or private, without regard to when they were contracted. This statute, after having been accepted by the people, and most of the State courts, as valid for a number of years, was, in 1869, attacked in the Supreme Court of the United States as unconstitutional. By a divided Court, the law in question was held "inconsistent with the spirit of the Constitution" and therefore, void. Three judges dissented. Then by the simple device of adding two judges to

[8] Ableman v. Booth and United States v. Booth, 21 Howard, 506.

[9] See discussion of Ableman v. Booth with explanatory note in *Selected Opinions of Chief Justices Dixon and Ryan of Wisconsin,* by Gilbert E. Roe, pp. 69–100.

[10] Hepburn v. Griswold, 8 Wallace, 603, and Knox v. Lee, 12 Wallace, 457.

the bench who were known to be favorable to the law, the question was again brought up and the law was held to be constitutional.[11]

The attempts of the courts to interfere with the reconstruction policy of the government following the Civil War and the disastrous consequences to the courts, is a familiar chapter of American History.[12] Concerning the tendency of the courts, during the last few years to again provoke a conflict with public sentiment, Prof. Haines, in concluding the chapters of his work just cited, says:

"The courts have been inevitably drawn into the social and economic conflicts arising in the course of our rapid industrial development, and there is an increasing number of instances in which judicial authority is being challenged in such a manner as to make it again the subject of political controversy."

If our discussion thus far has meant anything, it has shown that in the conflict between the masses of the people and the beneficiaries of special privilege, the courts have, according to popular belief, at least, ranged themselves on the side of the latter.

On the 20th of July last, an incident occurred in

[11] Legal Tender cases, 12 Wallace, 457.

[12] These cases are gathered together and discussed by Charles Grover Haines, in his chapter on "The Conflict Over Judicial Powers," in his *Studies in History, Economics and Public Law*, edited by the Faculty of Political Science, of Columbia University.

the Federal District Court in New York City which was widely commented upon by the press of the country as tending to prove that there was one law for the rich man and another for the poor one in the Federal Courts. It so happened that at the time in question, two men were sentenced for the crime of smuggling. Both sentences were imposed on pleas of guilty. One was a poor man, far gone with consumption, whose frauds on the government had been trifling. The other was a rich man, a member of a very large importing firm whose frauds on the government had run well over the million mark, and whose goods were sold to the fashionable trade throughout the country. The former received a prison sentence; the latter was merely fined twenty-five thousand dollars. I quote from one of the numerous editorials on this subject.[13]

"On July 20th, while he (the Federal Judge) sat in the United States District Court in New York, two men were brought up for sentence for smuggling. One was a comparatively small offender. He pleaded guilty to frauds on the Government in the weighing of importations of figs and cheese. The other was one of a syndicate of smugglers whose known and proved smuggling amounted to $1,400,000 worth of gowns and millinery goods. The little smuggler was sentenced to three months in prison. The big smuggler was discharged with a fine, $25,000, a fraction of what he had

[13] *Philadelphia North American*, Aug. 1, 1911.

swindled from the government. The United States District Attorney protested: 'I would rather see the defendant get one day in jail than be let off with a million-dollar fine. He visited my office and crawled on his knees and tried to kiss my hand in his efforts to get me to consent to a fine.' In addition to being a leader of a gang of rich smugglers, this defendant was a bail jumper."

The editorial, after referring to some further statements of the District Attorney to the effect that the defendant had tried in various way to reach him, concluded:

"We do not insist on the law's pound of flesh. We have no notion that the law should be vindictive. But on the same day that this million-dollar thief was set free on repayment of part of his stealings the same judge sent a poor little consumptive Greek to jail for frauds trifling in comparison."

In the same editorial, it is said:

"Once let the people be thoroughly convinced that their courts are not impartial, that there is one law for the rich and another for the poor and the seeds of revolution will have been sowed."

As a matter of fact, while the dramatic features attending the imposing of the above-mentioned sentences caused the affair to be generally commented upon in the press of the country, there was nothing unusual about it. The judge who imposed the sentences was quite within his right, and was well fortified by precedent for what he did. Fines for the rich law breaker and prison for the poor one is the general rule.

The distinction that was made by the New York Court in the afore-mentioned cases is being made every day in the year by the courts throughout the country. The distinction between the rich law breaker and the poor one, however, in the matter of the sentence imposed after conviction, is insignificant compared with the distinction the law makes between the poor man in the lawful pursuit of a living and the rich one engaged in adding to an already swollen fortune. The contest has begun for the control of the government as well as the natural resources of this country, between organized wealth and the individual demanding the right to live as a free man. Almost forty years ago, a great judge, in a memorable address,[14] thus foreshadowed the present crisis:

"There is looming up a new and dark power, I cannot dwell upon the signs and shocking omens of its advent. The accumulation of individual wealth seems to be greater than it ever has been since the downfall of the Roman Empire. And the enterprises of the country are aggregating vast corporate combinations of unexampled

[14] Address of Edward G. Ryan, Chief Justice of the Supreme Court of Wisconsin, delivered before the University of Wisconsin Law School, June, 1873.

capital, boldly marching, not for economic conquests only, but for political power. We see their colors, we hear their trumpets, we distinguish the sound of preparation in their camps. For the first time really in our politics, money is taking the field as an organized power. It is unscrupulous, arrogant, and overbearing. Already, here at home, one great corporation has trifled with the sovereign power and insulted the State. There is great fear that it and its great rival have confederated to make partition of the State and share it as spoils. Wealth has its rights. Industrious wealth has its honors. These it is the duty of the law to assert and protect, though wealth has great power of self-protection and influence beyond the limits of integrity. But money as a political influence is essentially corrupt; it is one of the most dangerous to free institutions; *by far the most dangerous to the free and just administration of the law.* It is entitled to fear, if not to respect: the question will arise, and arise in your day, though perhaps not fully in mine: Which shall rule — wealth or men; which shall lead — money or intellect; who shall fill public stations — educated and patriotic free men, or the feudal serfs of corporate capital?"

No one doubts that the struggle between wealth and men which Judge Ryan foresaw and eloquently predicted is upon us. The Anti-Trust law, the laws regulating public service corporations, and shortening the hours of labor, workmen's compensation laws and many similar measures, together with the movement for the conservation of our natural resources, and the attempts to break down our tariff wall, and the measures looking to the more direct control of the government by the people, such as direct primaries, the initiative, referendum and recall,— all these merely represent the efforts of the masses to break the grip which organized wealth has upon our government, and upon the natural resources of the country. They represent in part the beginning of the movement to free men from the dominion of corporate wealth and power. Where this conflict will lead us no man knows, but the courts seem already to have taken their position in it.

The decisions which I have herein reviewed constitute the reply which the courts have made and are making to this progressive movement. Unmindful of their experience in the past, they are again inviting a contest, the consequences of which must certainly be disastrous to them and possibly to the country as well. If these suggestions seem unduly pessimistic, I invite your attention to the language of one of the greatest jurists this country ever produced, whose opinions as Justice of the Missouri Court of Appeals are read and quoted wherever the common law prevails, and whose legal text-books are authority in every English-speaking Court in the world. I refer to Judge Seymour D. Thompson. In his address to the State Bar Association of Texas, in 1896, Judge Thompson reviewed the cases decided up to that time, showing the tendency of the courts to override and control the other departments of government and to protect property rights at the expense of human rights, and concluded his address as follows: [15]

"The dangerous tendencies and extravagant pretensions of the courts which I have pointed out ought not to be minimized, but ought to be resisted. Their resistance ought not to take place as advised by Jefferson, by 'meeting the invaders foot to foot,' but it ought to take place under the wise and moderate guidance of the legal profession, but the danger is that the people do not always so act. In popular governments, evils are often borne with stolid patience until a culminating point is reached, when the people burst into sudden frenzy and redress their grievances by violent and extreme measures, and even tear down the fabric of government itself. There is danger, real danger, that the people will see at one sweeping glance that all the powers of their government, Federal and State, lie at the feet of us lawyers, that is to say, at the feet of a judicial oligarchy; that those powers are being steadily exercised in behalf of the wealthy and powerful classes, and to the prejudice of the scattered and segregated people; that the power thus seized includes the power of amending the Constitution; the power of superintending the action, not merely of Congress, but also of the State Legislatures; the power of degrading the powers of the two houses of Congress, in making those investigations which they may deem accessory to wise

[15] *American Law Review*, Vol. XXX, pp. 697–9.

legislation, to the powers which an English court has ascribed to British Colonial legislatures; the power of superintending the judiciary of the States, of annulling their judgments and commanding them what judgments to render; the power of denying to Congress to raise revenue by a method employed by all governments; making the fundamental sovereign powers of government, such as the power of taxation, the subject of barter between corrupt legislatures, and private adventurers; holding that a venal legislature, temporarily vested with power, may corruptly bargain away those essential attributes of sovereignty and for all time; that corporate franchises bought from corrupt legislatures are sanctified and placed forever beyond recall by the people; that great trusts and combinations may place their yokes upon the necks of the people of the United States, who must groan forever under the weight, without remedy and without hope; that trial by jury and the ordinary criminal justice of the States, which ought to be kept near the people, are to be set aside, and Federal court injunctions substituted therefor; that those injunctions extend to preventing laboring men quitting their employment, although they are liable to be discharged by their employers at any time, thus creating and perpetuating a state of slavery. There is danger that the people will see these things all at once; see their enrobed judges doing their thinking on the side of the rich and powerful; see them look with solemn cynicism upon the sufferings of the masses, nor heed the earthquake when it begins to rock beneath their feet; see them present a spectacle not unlike that of Nero fiddling while Rome burns. There is danger that the people will see all this at one sudden glance, and that the furies will then break loose and that all hell will ride on their wings."

At the time this language was used the employers' liability law, the workmen's compensation law, and the laws regulating employment in various industries had not been nullified by the courts; neither had the most objectionable decisions been rendered against organized labor, and the courts had barely entered upon the work of destroying State statutes regulating great corporations. When one considers how the work of building up a Judicial Oligarchy has gone forward since Judge Thompson used the language quoted above, it must be admitted that we have steadily advanced toward the realization of the dangers he pointed out.

CHAPTER VII

SUGGESTIONS REGARDING REFORMS IN THE JUDICIARY

HOW not to reform the judiciary is quite as important as how to reform it. Even judges and lawyers freely admit the existence of abuses in our judicial system and the necessity of correcting them; but the remedy they generally suggest will aggravate the real evils, not correct them. The late Mr. Justice Brewer, for many years a member of the Supreme Court of the United States, and one of the most influential members of that body, in a statement published in the press of New York City, February 1, 1910, after referring to the popular dissatisfaction with the courts, had this to say:

"I advocate that the States enact laws that will permit of but one appeal after the trial judge. I have reached the conclusion that no judgment should be reversed upon a mere error in the admission of evidence, error in the ruling of the court, or in the trial judge's charge, unless it be clearly shown that such error worked a serious injustice upon the defendant. I maintain that laws should be passed which would give judges the necessary latitude in such matters to enable them to render quick justice. The laws of many of the Western

States are such that a judge is but little more than a moderator."

President Taft, in his message to the Sixty-first Congress, as we have seen, referred to what he called the "deplorable delay in the administration of civil and criminal law," which matters, he said, were receiving the attention of the Bar Associations of the country and the careful consideration of judges as well. His general recommendations were along the lines suggested by Mr. Justice Brewer, above quoted, and were the same in substance as the recommendations of the various Bar Associations of the country.

The recommendations of the Association of the Bar of the City of New York [1] are fairly typical of the recommendations emanating from courts and judges and Bar Associations generally on this subject. These recommendations (except as to some minor matters of practice) group themselves under three heads:

First: Those providing that the trial justice shall have greater power than heretofore in directing the jury to return a verdict in favor of one party or the other;

Second: Where, at the conclusion of the plaintiff's case, the Court is of the opinion plaintiff has not made out a cause of action and dismisses the complaint, this shall finally dispose of the case and

[1] See *New York Law Journal*, Jan. 6, 1910.

prevent the plaintiff bringing another action for the same cause;

Third: Where the judges now exercise the power to set aside a verdict if they are dissatisfied with it, but under the present practice must grant a new trial, they shall have power to direct what verdict shall be rendered.

The recommendations originating with judges, and lawyers' associations in the main, therefore, propose to increase the power of the judge, decrease the power of the jury and limit the right to appeal. These recommendations assume that the popular dissatisfaction with our courts involves only a matter of procedure, when, the fact is, it goes to the substance of judicial action.

The public complains less that decisions are a long time in coming than it does that they are wrong when they do come. I do not suppose that the Bar Associations and the judges by focusing attention upon the subjects of delay, expense, and reversals for technical causes, incident to our present judicial procedure, intend to divert public attention from the real abuses, although there may be some ungenerous enough to suggest that this is the explanation of the recommendations for judicial reform noticed above. It is easy to complain of the delay and expense of litigation; these are immediate evils and it is both popular and safe to rail against them. It would be better if we frankly admitted that great expense and considerable delay are inseparable from any litigation and that the wise thing for the prospective litigant to do is to settle his difficulties out of court without the aid of either judges or lawyers. It would, indeed, be strange if courts saw anything but good in an enlargement of their powers and lawyers are notoriously cowards where criticism of the courts is involved.

The real basis of complaint is not that judges haven't enough power, but that they have too much; it is not so much that litigation is costly as that its results are unsatisfactory; it is not that justice is delayed, but that it is denied. The purpose of the courts should not be so much to render speedy decisions as to give just judgments.

Underlying the whole argument of those advocates of judicial reform, whose contentions were ably stated by Mr. Justice Brewer in the quotation above given, is the assumption that when a decision is rendered, it is right. If this assumption were true the argument would be good and any change which would increase arbitrarily the power of the judges and hasten a judgment would be desirable. But if, on the other hand, the decisions of our courts where real and substantial contests occur are about as apt to be wrong as right, no very grave injury is likely to result if a decision is somewhat delayed and if such delay can guarantee a more nearly just result, it is desirable rather than otherwise.

In order to determine the proportion of our decisions likely to be wrong, according to the standards of the courts, even under our present so-called slow methods, which permit some time for consideration and deliberation, I have prepared certain tables of cases from various courts. The following table shows the fate of the cases reported in three volumes of the New York Appellate Division Reports. These reports were selected at random, covering different periods, but all sufficiently recent to show the conditions at the present time.

The Appellate Division of the New York Supreme Court is, it should be understood, an appellate court intermediate between the trial court and the Court of Appeals:

Total number of cases appealed:

Vol. 100 A. D.	257	
Vol. 105 A. D.	344	
Vol. 110 A. D.	431	1032

Total affirmances:

Vol. 100 A. D.	186	
Vol. 105 A. D.	234	
Vol. 110 A. D.	275	695

Total reversals:

Vol. 100 A. D.	71		
Vol. 105 A. D.	110		
Vol. 110 A. D.	156	337	1032

Affirmances: 67 per cent.
Reversals: 33 per cent.
Total number of cases appealed to Court of Appeals:

Vol. 100 A. D.	58	
Vol. 105 A. D.	66	
Vol. 110 A. D.	97	221

Of the cases appealed to the Court of Appeals substantially 20 per cent. were reversed and 80 per cent. were affirmed.

Practically none of the above cases were reversed on technical grounds, as New York has a very liberal statute requiring the courts to disregard technicalities not affecting the merits.

In 1903 a Commission was appointed by the Governor of the State of New York to inquire into the delays and expenses in the administration of justice in certain counties of the State of New York. This Commission made a most exhaustive report in 1904 and among other things summarized the results of the appeals to the Appellate Division for the years from 1896 to 1902 in the following table: [2]

[2] See New York Report of Commission on Law's Delays (1904), p. 25.

Year.	Affirmed Judgments.	Affirmed Orders.	Affirmed Total.	Reversed Judgments.	Reversed Orders.	Reversed Total.	Total Appeals.	Per cent. of Reversals.
1896	934	700	1634	441	376	817	2451	33.8
1897	874	771	1645	455	444	899	2544	35.3
1898	978	762	1740	519	454	973	2713	35.7
1899	1065	859	1924	487	412	899	2823	31.8
1900	1104	891	1995	472	395	867	2862	30.2
1901	1142	919	2061	467	378	845	2906	29.
1902	1152	934	2086	534	521	1055	3141	33.5
Total	7249	5856	13085	3375	2980	6355	19440	32.6

It will be observed that the last preceding table does not give the cases appealed from the Appellate Division to the Court of Appeals, but there is no reason to doubt that there would be at least as large a percentage of reversals as found in the three volumes of the reports referred to and tabulated first above.

I caused to be made also an examination of three volumes of the Wisconsin Supreme Court Reports, 50, 75, and 110 Wis., selecting them at random, to determine the number of cases therein which were affirmed and the number which were reversed. The following table shows the result of that examination:

Total number of cases appealed in the three volumes selected: 284

50 Wis.	Affirmances...........	59	
	Reversals.............	44	103

75 Wis.	Affirmances	67		
	Reversals	36	103	
110 Wis.	Affirmances	48		
	Reversals	30	78	284

Total affirmances:

50 Wis.	59		
75 Wis.	67		
110 Wis.	48	174	

Total reversals:

50 Wis.	44		
75 Wis.	36		
110 Wis.	30	110	284

Affirmances: 61 per cent.
Reversals: 39 per cent.
Appeals from verdict of jury:

	Affirmed	Reversed	Total	
50 Wis.	25	14	39	
75 Wis.	28	13	41	
110 Wis.	18	16	34	114

Appeals from decision of court:

	Affirmed	Reversed	Total		
50 Wis.	34	30	64		
75 Wis.	39	23	62		
110 Wis.	30	14	44	170	284

The judges of Wisconsin are at least equal in ability to those of any State in the Union, so that the above figures doubtless are fairly representative of the decisions in other States.

The above figures seem to show that more errors are committed by the trial court in matters decided without a jury than in those where a jury passes upon the facts.

In none of these tables is any account taken of the cases carried from the highest court of a State to the Supreme Court of the United States and there reversed. When it is considered that in most cases where there is a real contest, at least one appeal is taken, and that the questions which the appellate court can pass upon even under our present procedure are much restricted, and confined largely to questions of law, it is certain that a shockingly large number of cases are decided incorrectly even when those decisions are measured by the crude standards of right and wrong which the present rules of law prescribe.

Every wrong decision means that injustice and not justice was meted out by the court to the parties who came before it, that wrong and not right triumphed, that property was taken from one person and wrongfully transferred to another who had no claim upon it, or that the important personal rights of life, liberty and character were lost.

Limiting the right to appeal may conceal these wrongs, but it will not correct them. Greater haste in judicial action will hardly contribute to a wiser or a more just result. More arbitrary power vested in a judge may decrease the number of cases in which he can be reversed, but it will not make his wrong decisions right. It will only increase the number of wrong decisions and take away the possibility of correcting them.

By the law of averages, I suppose if litigants met together outside of court and settled their differences by drawing lots, the right would triumph half the time. Now when the result of judicial action, even with all the present opportunities for argument and consideration, fails to show a very much better average, it ought to be clear that hastening judicial proceedings will not give the desired results. The above considerations also ought to effectually dispose of the idea that our courts are other than very human institutions presided over by men with the faults and virtues, and prejudices and limitations, common to their fellows.

The first step toward bringing about better relations between the courts and the people is to subject the official acts of the judges to the same measure of criticism that is visited upon the acts of all other public officials.

If it is true, as charged, that our judges have stepped outside the judicial office and virtually become legislators, thereby usurping the functions of the law-making branch of the government, no language is strong enough to condemn such action and no proceeding too drastic, if it is necesssary, to correct the evil. No one will defend such action on the part of the judges or contend that a free government is posssible where judges exercise such power.

If, on the other hand, the charge is not true, then it is of the highest importance that the public be informed of the truth and that this ground of dissatisfaction with the judiciary be removed.

If it is true, as charged, that our judges generally are out of sympathy with the new and progressive views and policies of the present day, and are using the great powers of the judicial office to block and thwart the public will in these respects, and to preserve and extend the ancient but unjust privileges of wealth, contrary to the demands of a modern and enlightened public sentiment, then there is both just and serious ground of complaint against the courts.

But if this charge is untrue, the public interest requires that it shall be refuted at once.

Now this means discussion and freedom for discussion. It means that judicial decisions shall be subjected to the same public scrutiny that is applied to the votes and speeches of members of Congress or of the legislatures. It means that judges shall be put on a par with all others who hold commissions from the people to serve the public. The worst enemies of the courts and of the country are those who seek to prevent free criticism of judicial officers. To suggest a revolution as a means of avoiding an unpopular law passed by Congress and approved by the President would only provoke a smile, but President Hadley and Judge Thompson, and others like them point out as a grave danger that a revolution may be provoked by the unpopular rules of law laid down by the courts. Subject judges to the same measure of criticism and popular control that applies to the other officers mentioned and the difference in the public's attitude towards the two classes of officials will disappear. Respect for the courts and obedience to their decrees must rest upon some other basis than fear of a contempt proceeding or veneration for judicial mystery. The judge who mistakes damage to his vanity for an injury to the public proves his unfitness for judicial office.

Any legislation attempting to reform the judiciary which is not preceded by thorough discussion will at the best be ineffective and probably unwise and it is not impossible that a thorough discussion of the judicial abuses of which the public complains will render drastic legislation unnecessary.

It must be admitted, however, that judges at the present time are far too prone to secure themselves against unfavorable criticism by punishing as "contempt of court" wholesome and necessary comment and discussion of their official acts. Contempt of court has been not inaptly termed a "legal thumbscrew."[3] It is derived from the more ancient of-

[3] Oswald, *Contempt of Court* (1911), p. 5.

fense of contempt of king. As the king came to delegate some of his authority to his judges, the power to punish for contempt seems to have been delegated along with the authority. That the process of contempt is used to violate the fundamental guaranties of freedom of speech and of the press is freely charged, and it certainly is subject to great abuse.

A case previously cited in this volume presents a remarkable instance of the use of contempt proceedings to punish and prevent hostile criticism of the official conduct of a judge.[4] In that case it appears that Lindlay W. Morris was, in the fall of 1908, a candidate for reëlection for a fourth term as judge of the Ohio Court of Common Pleas in the judicial district of which Lucas County was a part. The campaign for Judge Morris' reëlection was largely made upon the proposition that he was a people's judge, and that he was opposed by corporations and trusts.[5] Charles A. Thatcher, a lawyer of large practice in the state of Ohio, extensively circulated literature during the campaign, claiming to prove from court records that the very contrary of the assertions made in behalf of Judge Morris was the truth. Among the statements that Thatcher circulated was the following:

"The attorneys who try the suits against the corporations are against Morris to a man. It isn't senti-

[4] *In re Thatcher*, 80 Ohio St. 492; *id.*, 83 Ohio St. 246.
[5] *Id.*, p. 633.

ment or politics with them. It is business. They never would be against Morris if he were a 'people's judge.'"

Concerning the circulation of this statement under the circumstances mentioned, the court said: [6]

"Whether he (Thatcher) wrote these words or not, he made himself responsible for them by distributing these circulars; and the peculiar methods of publishing them and the time at which it was done made them all the more inflammatory and dangerous. With a trumpeter and an automobile and the crippled Gravell, he went about gathering curious crowds and giving out harrowing stories of corruption, oppression and injustice, wrought in the name of the law. . . .

"The chief stress of the defense has been upon the claim that what the respondent did, and he denies very little, he did as a citizen and not as an attorney; and that as a citizen and an attorney he had the right, and it was his duty, to oppose a candidate whom he believed unfit for office. We concede that it is the duty of the bar to aid the public in the selection of proper persons for the bench; but that duty should be exercised *in subordination* to another duty, which is thus expressed in the code of ethics adopted by the American Bar Association. . . . 'Whenever there is proper ground for serious complaint of a judicial officer, it is the right and duty of the lawyer to submit his grievances to the *proper authorities*. In *such* cases, but *not otherwise*, such charges should be encouraged, and the person making them should be protected.' . . . If the judges

[6] *Id.*, p. 665.

who were attacked in these circulars were believed by the respondent to be guilty as he charges and insinuates, it was his privilege and duty to do what he could to have them impeached so that they might be deposed from office, when found guilty. As an attorney, or a citizen, he had the right to criticize the judgments and conduct of the judges in a decent and respectful manner; but no man has a right at any time to degrade and intimidate a public officer and bring his office into contempt by the publication of libelous matter imputing to him impeachable offenses, and the fact that the officer is a candidate for reëlection does not remove the ban."

In other words, if a judge is a candidate for reelection and has been guilty of offenses for which he could be impeached, or is believed to be guilty of such offenses, the facts relating to his alleged misconduct must not be published, and the only remedy is by impeachment proceedings to remove the offending judge from office.

The Court in disbarring Thatcher, apparently feeling that the contempt charges might be insufficient, based its judgment in part upon the alleged fact that he procured suit to be brought upon certain notes which had been paid and the cause of action thereon extinguished.[7] The suit on the notes which Thatcher advised to be brought was pending at the time the disbarment proceeding was heard in the Supreme Court.[8] After the decision of the Supreme Court disbarring

[7] *Id.*, p. 667. [8] *Id.*, p. 644.

Thatcher, the action on the notes was tried and it was judicially determined that the notes had not been paid and that the cause of action thereon had not been extinguished.[9]

The Legislature of the State of Ohio promptly took action in respect to the disbarment of Thatcher and passed an act overturning the judgment of the Supreme Court and reinstating Thatcher. Concerning the scene in the legislature when the bill reinstating Thatcher was passed, I quote from one of the leading newspapers of Columbus, Ohio:[10]

"Applauding a caustic criticism of the State Supreme Court, the house of representatives Thursday voted to reinstate Charles A. Thatcher, Toledo attorney, who was disbarred by the Supreme Court for alleged unprofessional conduct in criticizing Judge Morris of the Common Pleas court of Lucas County.

"The vote was 79 for Thatcher to 7 against. Those voting in the negative were Cowan, Langdon, Lewis, Pocock, Reid, Riddle and Speigel. Four of the seven are lawyers.

"The bill had already passed the senate and is now up to the governor for approval.

"Immediately following the passage of the bill by the house there were rumors that pressure was being

[9] My informant in respect to this statement is a reputable attorney of Toledo, Ohio, familiar with this litigation, but whose name I have not permission to use.

[10] *Columbus Citizen*, April 13, 1911.

brought to bear upon the chief executive to veto the bill.

"The vote on the bill in the house was attended by sensational and unprecedented features, in which Speaker Vining was forced to rap the house to order for applauding an arraignment of the Supreme Court judges. Representative Smith of Butler County touched off the fireworks in a speech urging the reinstatement of Thatcher. He related some untold history of the political pressure that was brought to bear to defeat the bill.

"'A messenger from the Supreme Court of Ohio called upon the judiciary committee, of which I am a member,' said Smith, 'with a request that the committee come over to the Supreme Court to discuss senate bill No. 70 and this Thatcher bill. We told the messenger that whenever the Supreme Court wished to call upon the committee it knew where our committee room was and we would be glad to give them the same hearing as we would any other citizen.' It was at this point that house members broke into applause.

"Continuing, Smith said the action of the Supreme Court was unprecedented. He followed with: 'The court in disbarring Thatcher sat upon its own case and rendered a verdict. Two members of the court, Justices Price and Shauck, were among the members criticized by Thatcher. Has it come to pass in Ohio when a citizen cannot exercise the constitutional right of free speech?' asked Smith, warming up to his subject.

"He pointed out that courts should not be above honest criticism.

"The Thatcher bill was backed principally by organized labor and a large number of attorneys."

It may be of interest to know that Judge Morris was defeated and that the bill to reinstate Thatcher became a law without the approval of the Governor.

Proceedings on the part of judges like those in the Thatcher case do more to breed contempt of court than all other causes combined. No charge against the judges, however untrue, could have so damaged the court in the public estimation or so impaired its usefulness as the court's own action in the premises had done.

If the courts do not speedily abandon the practice of punishing, under the guise of contempt proceedings, those who have merely incurred the displeasure of the judges, the Congress and State legislatures are likely to take the whole matter in hand and regulate the subject by statute and see to it that there shall be the same right to discuss the acts and abilities of judges that obtains in the case of other public servants.

While the emphasis in the present argument is placed on public discussion, agitation and education as a remedy for the popular distrust of the courts, it by no means follows that legislation should have no part in the programme. Indeed, proposed laws may be the best means of focusing public attention and crystallizing the discussion.

A noticeable example of this was furnished during the concluding days of the first session of the Sixty-second Congress, when Congress voted to admit Arizona as a state with a recall provision in her constitution which applied to judges as well as to other officers, and the President vetoed the measure solely because judges were not exempted from the recall provisions of the constitution.

The President in his veto message [11] gathered up and presented in the best possible form the objections to the recall of judges, but it is noticeable that no mention was made of the recall as applied to other officers and no objection urged against the Arizona constitution because it provided for the initiative and referendum as well as for the recall.

Nothing could bring out more clearly the rapid growth in public favor of these recent and radical measures than that they should all be passed over in silence except the recall as applied to judges. The recall provisions of the Arizona constitution as adopted by the people of that Territory and approved by Congress are given in the note.[12]

[11] *Cong.* Rec., Vol. XLVII (Aug. 15, 1911), p. 4111. The President's message was also published in the press of the country under the above date.

[12] Art. VIII. Sec. 1. Every public officer in the State of Arizona holding an elective office, either by election or appointment, is subject to recall from such office by the qualified electors of the electoral district from which candidates are elected to such office. Such electoral district may include

It may be assumed that President Taft in his veto message presented the arguments against the recall of judges in its best and most conclusive form since he had the advantage of the full and complete debates on the question which had just previously taken place

the whole state. Such number of said electors as shall equal 25 per cent. of the numbers of votes cast at the last preceding general election for all of the candidates for the office held by such officer may by petition, which shall be known as a recall petition, demand his recall.

Sec. 2. Every recall petition must contain a general statement, in not more than 200 words, of the grounds of such demand, and must be filed in the office in which petitions for nominations to the office held by the incumbent are required to be filed.

Sec. 3. If said officer shall offer his resignation, it shall be accepted, and the vacancy shall be filled as may be provided by law. If he shall not resign within five days after a recall petition is filed, a special election shall be ordered to be held, not less than 20 nor more than 30 days after such order, to determine whether such officer shall be recalled. On the ballots at said election shall be printed the reasons, as set forth in the petition, for demanding his recall, and, in not more than 200 words, the officer's justification of his course in office. He shall continue to perform the duties of his office until the result of said election shall have been officially declared.

Sec. 4. Unless he otherwise requests, in writing, his name shall be placed as a candidate on the official ballot without nomination. Other candidates for the office may be nominated to be voted for at said election. The candidate who shall receive the highest number of votes shall be declared elected for the remainder of the term. Unless the incumbent receive the highest number of votes, he shall be deemed to be removed from office upon qualification of his successor.

in the United States Senate. If the President in his message has presented the strongest arguments against the judicial recall features of the Arizona constitution, the country cannot but feel relief on reading the message, to discover that even if the recall will not accomplish much good, no substantial argument has been advanced to show that it can do any harm.

The argument against the recall of judges is the same as that against the recall of any other official and is all embodied in two propositions:

First: That the people will be so foolish on some occasions as to recall good judges.

Second: That judges will be intimidated, by fear of being recalled, into rendering improper decisions.

The first part of the argument is merely the world-old one that the masses are incapable of self-government.

The same argument which the President urged against this latest demand of democracy was made against its first demand in this country more than one hundred and thirty years ago, by Alexander Hamilton. The words used by the President and by Hamilton are almost identical and the idea is the same. Since the experience of more than a century and a quarter has shown that Hamilton's argument was entirely fallacious, it is not surprising that the same argument, even when advanced by the President and supported by the names of distinguished Senators creates no particular alarm. Writing in opposition to the election of the President by the people and in support of his election by the plan provided in the Constitution, of an Electoral College, by which it was intended to remove the Executive far from the popular will, Hamilton said:[13]

"It was equally desirable that the immediate election (of the President) should be made by men most capable of analyzing the qualities adapted to the station, and acting under circumstances favorable to deliberation, and to a judicious consideration of all the reasons and inducements which were proper to govern their choice. A small number of persons, selected by their fellow-citizens from the general mass, will be most likely to possess the information and discernment requisite to such complicated investigations."

Again, referring to the election of the President, Hamilton wrote:[14]

"The republican principle demands that the deliberate sense of the community should govern the conduct of those to whom they entrust the management of their affairs; but it does not require an unqualified compliance to *every sudden breeze of passion* or to every transient impulse which the people may receive from the arts of men, who flatter their prejudices to betray their interests."

[13] *The Federalist*, No. LXVIII, edited by Lodge, p. 424.
[14] *The Federalist*, No. LXXI, p. 446.

Referring to the recall provision of the Arizona constitution, President Taft on the 15th day of August, 1911, wrote this:[15]

"By the recall it is proposed to enable a minority of 25 per cent. of the voters of the district or state for no prescribed cause after a judge has been in office six months to submit the question of his retention in office to the electorate. The petitioning minority must say on the ballot what they can against him in 200 words and he must defend as best he can in the same space. . . . Could there be a system more ingeniously devised to subject judges to *momentary gusts of popular passion* than this?"

The striking similarity between the language of the President and of Hamilton is suggestive and leaves no room to doubt the identity of the idea. A few years, however, after Hamilton declared the people incapable of directly electing a President because they would be swayed by "every sudden breeze of passion," they, in spite of the Constitution, proceeded to elect the President directly and have continued to do so ever since and no man with any pretension to intelligence would now suggest a return to the method which Hamilton advocated.

The refutation of Hamilton's argument by the experience of more than a century is also a refutation

[15] *Cong. Rec.*, Vol. XLVII, p. 4112.

of the President's argument. There is no more reason to fear that "momentary gusts of popular passion" will sweep good men out of judicial office than there is to fear that a "sudden breeze of passion" will sweep bad men into the Executive office.

There is reason for more than a suspicion that Hamilton when he advanced this argument was not quite frank and that he did not believe in republican government at all. What he wrote in the *Federalist* was of course intended for all the public. What he said in the Constitutional Convention which sat with closed doors and conducted its proceedings with the utmost secrecy, evidently expressed his real view. The notes of the Constitutional Convention, secretly taken by Madison and published long after the death of every one connected with it, reports Hamilton as follows: [16]

"In his *private* opinion he had no scruple in declaring, supported as he was by the opinion of so many of the wise and good, that the British government was the best in the world, and that he doubted much whether anything short of it would do in America. He hoped gentlemen of different opinions would bear with him in this and begged them to recall the change of opinion on this subject which had taken place and was still going on."

[16] *Journal of Constitutional Convention*, by Madison, pp. 181–2.

Again, in the same convention, he said:

"To the proper adjustment of it (conflicting interests) the British owe the excellence of their constitution. *Their House of Lords is a most noble institution,* having nothing to hope for by a change, and a sufficient interest by means of their property, in being faithful to the national interest, they form a permanent barrier against every pernicious innovation, whether attempted on the part of the Crown or the Commons."

As is well known also, Hamilton contended that the United States Senate should be a permanent body and that the President should hold for life.[17] Again: [18]

"He acknowledged himself not to think favorably of republican government; but addressed his remarks to those who did think favorably of it in order to prevail on them to tone their government as high as possible."

Hamilton also held other rather undemocratic views. In his report as Secretary of the Treasury to the House of Representatives, December 5, 1791, concerning manufactories, he said: [19]

"It is worthy of remark that in general women and children are rendered more useful and the latter more

[17] *Id.*, pp. 182, 183.
[18] *Id.*, p. 244.
[19] *Works of Alexander Hamilton,* edited by Lodge, p. 314.

early useful by manufacturing establishments than they would otherwise be. Of the number of persons employed in the cotton manufactories of Great Britain it is computed that four-sevenths nearly are women and children, of whom the greatest proportion are children and many of them of a tender age, and thus it appears to be one of the attributes of the manufactories and one of no small consequence to give occasion to the exertion of a greater quantity of industry even by the same number of persons where they happen to prevail than would exist if there was no such establishment."

That Hamilton could not have been ignorant of the horrible conditions under which women and children were enslaved by the English factory system which he commended is shown by the fact that in 1784 public attention had been drawn to these conditions by the report of a Commission of Inquiry.[20]

While it may be that Madison's journal reporting Hamilton's real views expressed as he supposed, in secret, placed beside what he wrote in the *Federalist* for the public, shows him to have been something of a hypocrite, it makes clear his reasons for declaiming against the danger of the people's being swayed by "every sudden breeze of passion." Why the same argument should be made at the present time by genuine believers in popular government is more difficult to understand. They have less reason for making it than Hamilton had, since the patience and

[20] *Encyclopedia Britannica*, Vol. XVI, p. 10.

moderation with which the people have conducted their affairs since the formation of this government is a complete answer to the Hamiltonian argument.

The people heard their Supreme Court, in the Dred Scott case, declare negro slavery a national institution, and they were obliged to wash that decision off the records of the government with the best blood of the nation, and yet they did not rend the court.

They heard the same court in the Legal Tender cases deny them the means of preserving the country from bankruptcy and financial ruin, and they did no violence to the court, but merely resorted to the subterfuge of packing it with some new judges who changed the decision.

In later years the Supreme Court in the Income Tax cases denied the people the right, which every other government on earth possesses, of placing the burden of taxation upon the rich instead of the poor, but the people have obeyed the decision, and ever since it was rendered have been trying with almost Job-like patience to amend the Constitution so as to escape from the unjust judgment of the court.

Within a very short time the people have seen the Supreme Court in the Standard Oil and Tobacco Trust cases greatly weaken the Anti-Trust law, to which they looked for relief from the exactions of monopoly, and while they are seeking means to restore the law to its former efficacy, their language is more temperate than that used by the minority of the Court in those cases.

These are only a few instances in which the people have remained calm in the face of provocation which seemed intended to test their capacity for self-restraint. These facts may support the argument that the judicial recall when available will be too seldom used, but they make it seem truly marvelous that any one can read the history of patience and forbearance on the part of the masses and then distrust them for fear that they may give way to "momentary gusts of popular passion." It is difficult to believe that any judge who was conscious of good motives and of rectitude in his official acts would have the slightest fear of ever being removed from office by a people who have manifested such patience with their public officers. This clearly seems to have been the view taken by a majority of the members of the Congress, as shown by their speeches, as well as by their votes.[21]

The other half of the argument against the recall of judges, namely that the possession of such power

[21] Sen. Owen, *Cong. Rec.*, Vol. XLVII (Aug. 4, 1911), p. 3687; Sen. Poindexter, *Cong. Rec.*, Vol. XLVII (Aug. 7, 1911), p. 3801; Sen. Bourne, *Cong. Rec.*, Vol. XLVII (Aug. 5, 1911), p. 3811; Sen. Clapp, *Cong. Rec.*, Vol. XLVII (Aug. 8, 1911), p. 3839.

The United States Senate passed the resolution admitting Arizona with the judicial recall provision in the Constitution by a vote of 53 to 18 (*Cong. Rec.*, Vol. XLVII, p. 3856).

by the people will intimidate the courts into making wrong decisions, has, if possible, less to support it than that already considered, and is, besides, the severest arraignment ever made of the judiciary of this country. If it is true that judges will serve the power that controls the tenure of their office to the extent of rendering wrong decisions when that power is the people, is it not true that they will be equally subservient to any other power which controls their official life?

It is common knowledge that the people have practically nothing to do with the appointment of a federal judge or with his retention in office after his appointment. Concerning the appointment of federal judges, United States Senator Robert L. Owen, in the speech cited above, said they were:

> "nominated, and proposed, and urged, and appointed through the influence of special interests. Their decisions will continue to reflect their honest previous predilections and bias by virtue of which they were nominated."

United States Senator Moses E. Clapp, in his speech cited above, said:

> "We cannot be blind to the fact that in spite of the average high purposes, a sinister influence seeks to dominate our political life, securing both the election and appointment of officers, *judicial* and otherwise, favorably inclined to its interests."

But the influence which controls the appointment of the federal judge does not stop at that point. In the usual course of events there has been a steady progression in the federal judiciary from district judge to circuit judge, with an assignment to court of appeals work, and with an appointment to the Supreme bench as a possible goal. If a judge can be swerved from a straight course by any power because it controls his official destiny, the Federal judiciary system was admirably designed to serve the interests of the wealthy and powerful classes.

While the argument in favor of the recall of an elective State judge may not be as strong as in the case of federal judges, there is no particular argument against it, and certainly none that does not apply to all other State officers.

It must always be remembered that only a small portion of the work of a judge consists in settling the rights of the private individuals who come before him as litigants. As titles to real property become more and more settled and the principles of business contracts fixed, this litigation becomes less in volume and in importance.

The litigation of this country is becoming more and more quasi-political in character, involving questions of governmental policy concerning which the people have the same right to be heard that they have when the Congress passes upon the same or similar measures. That the people will make mistakes in attempting to secure control of the judiciary through the medium of the recall and the election of the federal judges is to be expected. But every advance in popular government has been made in the same way and the same arguments that are made against this movement now, have been made against every effort of the masses to acquire some share in government. No judge was ever defeated for reëlection, and none will ever be recalled because of an erroneous decision involving only the private rights of individual litigants.

In 1911 occurred the first, and up to the present writing, the only attempt to recall a judge. The attempt grew out of the trial of the case of the State v. McClallen, which occurred in Rosenburg, Oregon, in May, 1911. The facts are sufficiently set forth in the recall petition, which was in part as follows:

"We, the undersigned citizens and legal voters of the State of Oregon, and of the Second Judicial District (consisting of the counties of Douglas, Lane, Coos, Curry, Benton and Lincoln), respectfully demand the recall of Circuit Judge John S. Coke of said Second Judicial District; and each for himself says: I have personally signed the petition; I am a legal voter of the State of Oregon and of the Second Judicial District thereof; my residence and post office are correctly written after my name."

Then followed a statement of the reasons for the proposed recall wherein the Judge was charged with unfairness in the conduct of the trial.

Signatures were obtained to the petition in the vicinity where the crime was committed and the trial occurred, but the petition met with little popular favor and was abandoned because the vast majority of voters refused to sign it, believing that the Judge was honest, however much mistaken he may have been.

This case presented every feature necessary to call forth one of those "momentary gusts of popular passion" from which the opponents of the recall would protect our judges; but the popular passion was not present. While the people of that community were strongly in favor of the recall as applied to judges, they simply did not feel that a situation had arisen which made the use of the recall necessary.[22]

The recall of judges is to be carefully distinguished from another idea, which is supported by some men of prominence, and which has come to be described as the "recall of judicial decisions." The former may be applied without materially departing from our constitutional form of government;

[22] For full account of the effort to secure signatures to the petition to recall Judge Coke, see article by Judson King, in *La Follette's Weekly Magazine* of November 25, 1911.

the latter is absolutely destructive of the constitution. The recall of Judges merely means that where a Judge has shown, from any cause, that he is not discharging the functions of the judicial office in fundamental and important matters, as the people desire, he will be discharged and a new judge possessing the necessary technical qualifications selected in his place. The recall of judicial decisions means that the wholly untrained layman shall undertake to do, personally, the highly specialized and technical work of a judge. The great vice in this idea, however, is that it would be used as a means of amending the Constitution by a majority vote. It would soon come about that laws would be passed, simply for the purpose of having them declared unconstitutional, and then by a popular vote overturning the decision of the Court, and in that respect amend the Constitution. The Constitution, therefore, would be immediately reduced to the level of a statute, since any portion of it could be amended, or repealed, at any time by a mere majority of the popular vote. While there is little likelihood of this idea finding a permanent place in the minds of the people, that any one should be found, who seriously advocates this idea, is significant of the extent to which the dissatisfaction with the courts has gone, and ought to show the necessity of reforming the courts, along lines less revolutionary.

In 1891 Judge Seymour D. Thompson had this to say concerning the popular election of federal judges:[23]

"If the proposition to make the federal judiciary elective instead of appointive is once seriously discussed before the people, nothing can stay the growth of that sentiment and it is almost certain that every session of the federal Supreme Court will furnish material to stimulate that growth."

But whether federal judges shall be elected or appointed or whether all judges shall be subject to the recall, are merely questions of method. The one fact concerning the judiciary which is now coming to be generally understood is this: The Judicial Department of the government is the only one which has successfully resisted the modern movement towards Democracy.

The Electoral College provided by the Constitution, by which the selection of the President and Vice-President was intended to be taken out of the hands of the people, has been superseded by the direct popular election of those officials. The constitutional plan of making the United States Senate represent the property interests and financial forces of the country by giving to the members of that body long terms and providing for their election by the legislatures of the several States, is being overthrown

[23] 25 *Am. Law Review*, p. 288.

and election of United States senators by a direct vote which is already a fact in many States, will soon be enforced in all. Already this change has revolutionized the character of the United States Senate and bids fair to make it a body more representative of the people than the House of Representatives. The judicial branch of the government alone has yielded nothing of its constitutional powers to the popular will, but on the contrary, it has extended its own power far beyond what even the framers of the Constitution contemplated, and this it has done without any substantial basis for its power.

It has passed almost without comment that by a law which took effect January 1st, 1912, every United States Circuit Court was abolished. True, the powers theretofore exercised by those courts, were transferred in the main to the United States District Courts, but the power to abolish the Circuit Courts was nevertheless exercised by Congress. Every United States Circuit Court, below the Supreme Court, was created by Congress, and in consequence can be abolished by it, or the judges thereof made elective, while even the Supreme Court depends for the substance of its power upon Congressional action. The Constitution provides, Sec. 1, Art. III:

"The judicial power shall be vested in one Supreme Court and in such inferior courts as the Congress may from time to time ordain and establish."

The number of members of which the Court shall be composed is wholly a matter of legislation, and so to a large extent are the more important powers which the Court exercises.[24]

Under these circumstances, it is folly for the courts to engage in a contest with the legislative branch of the Government. The recall which the people would seldom or never exercise, is much less of a menace to the dignity and prestige of the courts than Congressional action, when provoked by arbitrary acts of the judiciary. For example, the statute above referred to which codifies the laws relating to the judiciary, approved March 3d, 1911, and which took effect January 1st, 1912, in Sec. 21 of Chapter I thereof provides:

"*Whenever* a party to any action or proceeding, civil or criminal, shall make and file an affidavit that the judge before whom the action or proceeding is to be tried or heard has a personal bias or prejudice, either against him or in favor of any opposite party to the suit, such judge *shall proceed no further therein,* but another judge shall be designated in the manner prescribed in the section last preceding, or chosen in the manner prescribed in section twenty-three, to hear such matter. Every such affidavit shall state the facts and the reasons for the belief that such bias or prejudice ex-

[24] Sec. 2, Art. III, U. S. Constitution. Barry v. Mercein, 5 How. 103, 119; In re McCardle, 7 Wall. 506, 513; In re Vidal, 179 U. S. 126.

ists, and shall be filed not less than ten days before the beginning of the term of the Court, or good cause shall be shown for the failure to file it within such time. No party shall be entitled in any case to file more than one such affidavit; and no such affidavit shall be filed unless accompanied by a certificate of counsel of record that such affidavit and application are made in good faith."

Shortly after this statute went into effect, an affidavit of prejudice was offered for filing in the case of the State of Delaware v. Glascow, in the United States District Court at Wilmington, Del., by counsel in behalf of the defendant. The affidavit of prejudice was offered after the defendant had been convicted, and before he was sentenced, but at the earliest date possible under the law, and was apparently designed to prevent sentence being imposed by the Judge who tried the case. The United States District Judge held that the statute in question could not apply to the case in the stage which it had reached, and also refused to permit the filing of the affidavit at all. After denouncing defendant and defendant's counsel for presenting the affidavit, the Judge said:

" And what accentuates the ingratitude and baseness of such an assault upon the judicial reputation of one who, whatever his failings or shortcomings, has always tried to be fair and impartial as between litigants in the administration of justice, criminal and civil, is the fact that if section 21 of the act in question be applicable to this case, which as the court has determined it is not, the judge has no protection whatever against a false and perjured affidavit, and his reputation as a fair and impartial dispenser of justice goes for nothing, and is absolutely at the mercy of any litigant who, either of his own motion or at the instigation of unscrupulous counsel charges bias or prejudice against him. The mouth of the judge is sealed; he is not permitted to deny or refute the allegations made against him, whatever may be their falsity or whatever his reputation as a just and impartial judge, or howsoever gross the depravity of the affiant. On the above assumption, upon the filing of such an affidavit the judge, without any opportunity for a hearing on the question of his alleged bias or prejudice, is summarily removed from the case on the ground of bias or prejudice and his reputation, which is his property and most valued possession, blasted in the eyes of the community, who, without understanding the peculiar character of the law under which the judge is removed, but knowing that he has been accused of bias or prejudice, naturally conclude that such a charge has been satisfactorily established against him when, in point of fact his mouth and the mouths of witnesses on whom he might otherwise rely, are absolutely sealed. But this court cannot impute to Congress an intent that a convicted felon should be able to oust the judge before whom he was tried from further proceeding in the case.

"It is abhorrent to one's sense of justice that judicial reputations should be at the mercy of convicted criminals whose false affidavits the judges are not permitted to refute. A judge's reputation is his property, of which he should not be deprived without due process of law. The affidavit in question is false, insulting and malicious, and, as it is unauthorized by the law, it has no proper place among the files of this court."

The foregoing statement of the learned Justice seems to be a correct, if somewhat intemperate, interpretation of the statute discussed. The purpose of the statute seems to be exactly what the judge declared it to be. In fairness to the Congress, however, it must be assumed that only grave abuses would have called forth such a statute. The recall with all of its requirements insuring delay, discussion, full public hearings, careful consideration, and finally the deliberate action of thousands of voters, is an extremely mild method of removing a judge, compared with the method provided by the Congress in the above quoted statute.

It must be expected that the conflict with the courts will be a hard one, for the judiciary is undoubtedly looked upon as the last and final bulwark of Special Privilege. If the judges will retrace their steps and for the future exercise only constitutional powers, it is probable that their jurisdiction will long be left unquestioned. If they will never declare a statute unconstitutional unless it is so plainly so that any person of intelligence, whether a lawyer or not, can see it, they will find that all the people are willing that the Constitution shall be placed above any statute. It should not take a lawyer to determine in a given case whether two plainly written provisions of law — one a constitution, the other a statute — conflict or not, and if the question of whether there is a conflict is so doubtful that judges divide almost equally upon it, the people have a right to believe that it is not the Constitution, but the preconceived notions of the judges with which the statute conflicts.

If the courts will interpret statutes according to the intention of the law-making branch of the government, without reference to their own economic or social theories, and fully recognize the right of the people within plain constitutional limits, to make such laws as they please, another great cause of popular discontent will be removed. But if the courts as now constituted, will not do these things voluntarily, then they will be reconstructed and forced to do them. The recall and also the popular election of all judges for short terms seem at this time measures likely to be adopted in an effort to force the courts back into their original constitutional position where they will serve the interests and protect the rights of the whole people.

TABLE OF CASES

T

U

V

W

Y

INDEX

A

B

C

D

E

F

G

H

I

J

K

L